Teaching Children Tawheed

- A guide to what is obligatory upon us to teach our Children -

By the Noble Imaam & Reviver

Shaykh Muhammad bin 'Abdul-Wahhaab

[d.1206H]

Followed by

Examples from the Qur'aan, the Sunnah and the Statements of the Salaf related to raising Children

Translated by Aboo Sufyaan 'Uthmaan Beecher

Reviewed by *Shaykh* Aboo 'Uthmaan Muhammad al-'Anjaree

ISBN 978-1-4507-0125-9

First Edition   1430AH/2009

© Copyright 2009

All Rights Reserved. No part of this publication may be reprinted, reproduced or utilized in any form or by any means, electronic, mechanical, photocopying, recording or otherwise without the express permission of the copyright owner.

Front & Back Cover Design:	Aboo Sufyaan & Irfan Mug'd
Front Cover Photo:	Audrey Marsolais
Back Cover Photo:	Irfan Mug'd

Noor Al-Furqaan Publications

www.nooralfurqaan.com

Send inquiries or comments to:

TeachingChildrenTawheed@gmail.com

Contents

Introduction 1

First page of the manuscript in Egypt 3

Teaching Children Tawheed by Imaam Muhammad bin 'Abdul-Wahhaab 4

Examples from the Qur'aan, the Authentic Sunnah and Statements of the Salaf Related to raising Children 33

A Comfort for the Eyes 34

Giving the Children a Good Beginning 36

Establishing a conducive environment for Children in the home 40

Showing Love, Affection and Mercy towards the Children 42

Good treatment towards ones Children and providing for them and fulfilling their Rights 47

Good treatment towards the Orphans and providing for them and taking care of their needs 53

Teaching Children *Tawheed* and the Correct *'Aqeedah* 56

Teaching Children the Danger of Innovation in the *Deen* and Protecting them from it 59

Encouraging the Children upon Acts of Worship and Obedience 63

Encouraging the Children upon Seeking Knowledge 67

Supplicating for the Children and Greeting them and Conveying *Salaam* to them 71

Kindness and Good Manners towards the Children and being patient with them 75

Justice between the Children 78

Cultivating the Children upon Good Manners and Etiquettes 79

Marrying off ones Daughters 84

Dealing with the Children during the Prayer 86

Allowing the Children to play 88

Keeping the Children inside at the time of Maghrib 89

Verily among your Wives and your Children there are Enemies for you 91

A Final Note from Ibnul-Qayyim 94

Introduction

Verily all praise is due to Allaah, and may His peace and blessings be upon His final Messenger Muhammad, and upon his family and his Companions one and all. To proceed:

Before the noble reader – may Allaah guide him or her to that which He is pleased with – is the translation of a short but concise treatise by the great *Imaam* and reviver, *Shaykhul-Islaam* Muhammad bin 'Abdul-Wahhaab – may Allaah have mercy upon him, entitled "**Teaching Children Tawheed** *(Ta'leemus-Sibyaan at-Tawheed)*". It was written by the *Imaam*– may Allaah have mercy upon him – to direct us to those matters which we must teach our children, comprising important fundamentals of the *Deen* (Religion) of Islaam, written in the form of questions and answers. And as is always found in the writings of *Imaam* Muhammad bin 'Abdul-Wahhaab, he brings the proofs for these matters from the Book of Allaah, the Sunnah of His Messenger (ﷺ), and the statements of our *Salafus-Saalih* (Pious Predecessors).

This book is based on a manuscript found in Egypt and has not been found in any of the collections of the *Imaam*'s works. A copy of this manuscript is housed in Markaz ash-Shaybaanee in Kuwait. It was transcribed from an older print and re-published by Daar al-Haramayn but with several mistakes. It was then checked against the manuscript copy as well as additional manuscripts and corrected by our brothers Aboo Muhammad Fawaaz al-'Awwadee and Aboo 'Abdil-Muhsin Muhammad al-Mansour – may Allaah reward both of them with good. The treatise was then translated using their corrected transcriptions of the manuscript. All footnotes and references are theirs except for those that have been added to clarify or add additional benefit to something in the text, or to provide the proof or reference for a point that the *Imaam* – may Allaah have mercy upon him – mentions.

The translation was reviewed by Sulaymaan ar-Roomee and Yoosuf bin Sayf and the book proofread in it's entirety by 'Umar Lewis – may Allaah reward them all for their time and effort.

And may Allaah reward our noble *Shaykh*, Aboo 'Uthmaan Muhammad al-'Anjaree – may Allaah preserve him- for sitting with me on numerous occasions to read through the Arabic text and the English translation, and for pointing out valuable benefits and principles to help clarify many points in the text for the reader. May Allaah bless him for his support and tireless efforts in clarifying the correct, clear methodology of the *Salaf*. It was by his direction and advice that the second section of this book was compiled and the explanatory footnotes were added, and all praise is due to Allaah.

Likewise, I must thank our *Shaykh*, Aboo 'Abdir-Rahmaan Taariq as-Subay'ee and our *Shaykh* Aboo Muhammad Ahmad as-Subay'ee for their valuable advice, comments and encouragement.

And I would like to thank my wife Umm Sufyaan for her patience and constant support.

I ask Allaah to accept it from us and all those who aided in its preparation and publication as being sincerely for His Sake and place it in our scales of good deeds. *Aameen*.

Aboo Sufyaan 'Uthmaan bin William Beecher
5 Rajab, 1430 H/28 June, 2009
Kuwait

First page of the manuscript in Egypt

Teaching Children Tawheed

The noble *Imaam*, the Reviver and Caller to *Tawheed*[1], *Shaykhul-Islaam* Muhammad bin 'Abdul-Wahhaab – may Allaah the Most High have mercy upon him – said:

"I seek refuge in Allaah from the accursed Shaytaan. I begin with the Name of Allaah, the Most Merciful, the Bestower of Mercy.
Verily all praise is due to Allaah, we praise Him, we seek His Aid and we seek His forgiveness. And we seek refuge in Allaah from the evils of our own selves and from our evil

---

[1] *Tawheed* linguistically means to make something one. In its Islaamic meaning, it means to worship Allaah Alone, singling Him out in every act of worship, and to abandon the worship of anything other than Him, and this is the meaning of *Laa ilaaha illallaah*. And *Tawheed* also has a more general definition, which is the three categories of *Tawheed*:
  (1) *Tawheed ar-Ruboobiyyah*, the Oneness of Allaah in His Lordship, which is to single out Allaah in His Actions. So He Alone is the Creator and Sustainer, and He Alone gives life and death and Allaah Alone arranges the affairs of His creation.
  (2) *Tawheed al-Uloohiyyah*, or the Oneness of Allaah in His sole right to be worshipped, which is to single out Allaah with our acts of worship. So we direct all of our actions of worship, whether they be actions of the limbs, the heart or the tongue to Allaah Alone without directing anything from them to other than Him. And this was the *da'wah* of every Prophet and Messenger to their peoples.
  (3) *Tawheed al-Asmaa' was-Sifaat*, or the Oneness of Allaah in regards to His Beautiful Names and Lofty, Perfect Attributes. So Allaah is perfect and totally incomparable to His creation. His Attributes are attributes of perfection, free from every deficiency. We affirm them as they come in the Book and the authentic Sunnah without negating them, distorting or changing their meanings, comparing them to those of the creation, and without asking 'how' they are.
Refer to "Explanation of the Three Fundamental Principles" by *Shaykh* Muhammad bin Saalih al-'Uthaymeen [pg. 71-74] for more. {Translator}

actions. Whomever Allaah guides, there is none who can lead him astray, and whomsoever Allaah leads astray, there is no guide for him. I bear witness that nothing has the right to be worshipped [in truth] except Allaah Alone, without any partner, and I bear witness that Muhammad is His slave and Messenger (ﷺ). To proceed:

So this beneficial treatise is in regards to what is obligatory upon the human being to teach the children, before teaching them the Qur'aan [2], so he becomes a person who is complete,

---

[2] What the *Imaam* shows here —may Allaah have mercy upon him – is that teaching children *Tawheed* comes first. So for parents, the first and most important thing for them to instill in their children's hearts is *Tawheed*. And this is what the Messenger (ﷺ) did with the children, like Ibn 'Abbaas, when he (ﷺ) said: *"O young man, I shall teach you some words [of advice]: Be Mindful of Allaah and Allaah will protect you. Be Mindful of Allaah and you will find Him in front of you. If you ask, then ask Allaah [Alone]; and if you seek help, then seek help from Allaah [Alone]. And know that if the Ummah were to gather together to benefit you with anything, they would not benefit you except with what Allaah had already prescribed for you. And if they were to gather together to harm you with anything, they would not harm you except with what Allaah had already prescribed (decreed) for you. The Pens have been lifted and the Pages have dried."* [Collected by at-Tirmidhee (#2516) and *Shaykh* al-Albaanee declared it to be authentic] And Jundub bin 'Abdillaah said: "We were with the Prophet (ﷺ) and we were youth who had grown strong (in body), so we learned *Eemaan* before we learned the Qur'aan, then we learned the Qur'aan and it increased us in *Eemaan*." [Collected by Ibn Maajah (#61) and declared authentic by *Shaykh* al-Albaanee] And from the lives of the Companions – in the authentic narrations – we can understand the meanings of the Qur'aan and Sunnah. {Translator}

upon the *fitrah* ³ of Islaam, and a good, firm *muwwahid* (person of *Tawheed*) upon the path of *Eemaan* (true, correct faith). And I arranged it upon the way of questions and answers:

---

³ The *Fitrah* is the natural state and inclination that Allaah created the human being upon, which is the innate belief in Allaah and that He Alone is the Creator and Sustainer, and that He Alone is to be worshipped. The Messenger of Allaah (ﷺ) said: **"There is no child born except that he is upon the Fitrah. So it is his parents who make him a Jew or a Christian or a Magian."** [al-Bukhaaree in the Book of *Tafseer* (#4775)] And this *hadeeth* shows that the Parents are the first step for the guidance of the children towards the right path or the wrong path. So parents are responsible to guide them to *Tawheed* from the very beginning. {Translator}

Question 1: If it is said to you: Who is your *Rabb* (Lord)?

Answer: Then say: My *Rabb* (Lord) is Allaah.

Question 2: And what is the meaning of *ar-Rabb*?

Answer: Then say: The Owner of Dominion who is worshipped [4], the One who aids and supports, the Creator and Sustainer, Allaah, the sole-possessor of the right to be worshipped and of servitude over His creation.

Question 3: So if it is said to you: How did you come to know your Lord?

Answer: Then say: I know Him by His *aayaat* (signs) and His *makhlooqaat* (creation). And from His *aayaat* are the night and the day, and the sun and the moon. And from His *makhlooqaat* are the heavens and the earth and (all) that is in them. And the *daleel* (proof) for that is His saying, the Most High:

إِنَّ رَبَّكُمُ ٱللَّهُ ٱلَّذِى خَلَقَ ٱلسَّمَٰوَٰتِ وَٱلْأَرْضَ فِى سِتَّةِ أَيَّامٍ ثُمَّ ٱسْتَوَىٰ عَلَى ٱلْعَرْشِ يُغْشِى ٱلَّيْلَ ٱلنَّهَارَ يَطْلُبُهُۥ حَثِيثًا وَٱلشَّمْسَ وَٱلْقَمَرَ وَٱلنُّجُومَ

---

[4] *Imaam* Muhammad bin 'Abdul-Wahhaab said in his *Thalaathatul-Usool*: "So if it is said to you: Who is your Lord?, then say: My Lord is Allaah, Who nurtures me and nurtures all of the creation with His blessings. He is my *Ma'bood* (the One that I worship), I have no other *ma'bood* except Him." {Translator}

$$\text{مُسَخَّرَاتٍ بِأَمْرِهِ أَلَا لَهُ الْخَلْقُ وَالْأَمْرُ تَبَارَكَ اللَّهُ رَبُّ الْعَالَمِينَ}$$

"Indeed your Lord is Allaah, Who created the heavens and the earth in Six Days, and then He *Istawaa* (rose over) the Throne (really in a manner that suits His Majesty). He brings the night as a cover over the day, seeking it rapidly. And (He created) the sun, the moon, the stars subjected to His Command. Surely, His is the Creation and Commandment." [5]

Question 4: So if it is said to you: For what (purpose) did He create you?

Answer: Then say: To worship Him Alone, without associating any partner with Him (in worship), and obedience to Him by carrying out what He ordered, and abandoning what He prohibited, as Allaah the Most High said:

$$\text{وَمَا خَلَقْتُ الْجِنَّ وَالْإِنسَ إِلَّا لِيَعْبُدُونِ}$$

"And I (Allaah) did not create the jinn and mankind except that they should worship Me (Alone)." [6]

And as He said, the Most High:

---

[5] Al-A'raaf (7):54
[6] adh-Dhaariyah (51):56

$$\text{وَاعْبُدُوا اللَّهَ وَلَا تُشْرِكُوا بِهِ شَيْئًا}$$

"And worship Allaah (Alone) and join none with Him in worship" [7]

And *shirk* is the greatest sin by which Allaah is disobeyed, as He said, the Most High:

$$\text{إِنَّهُ مَن يُشْرِكْ بِاللَّهِ فَقَدْ حَرَّمَ اللَّهُ عَلَيْهِ الْجَنَّةَ وَمَأْوَاهُ النَّارُ}$$

"Verily, whosoever sets up partners in worship with Allaah, then Allaah has forbidden Paradise for him, and the Fire will be his abode." [8]

And *shirk* is that a person makes a rival for Allaah, calling upon (it), and hopes in it, or fears it, or places his trust and reliance upon it, or has fervent desire towards it besides Allaah, and other than that from the various types of acts of

---

[7] an-Nisaa' (4):36
[8] al-Maa'idah (5):72

worship [9]. For indeed, *'Ibaadah* (worship) is: a comprehensive term for everything that Allaah loves and is pleased with from speech and actions, inward and outward. [10]

And from them (those acts of worship) is *ad-Du'aa* (supplication). And the Most High said:

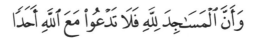

"And the mosques are for Allaah (Alone), so do not invoke anyone along with Allaah." [11]

---

[9] We must be very cautious of *shirk* and ingrain fear of it into ourselves and our children. And it is upon us to know and beware of all of its avenues, because *shirk* enters upon the people in small ways that are not obvious to them and through acts that they do not know are acts of *shirk*, for example placing an "eye" or a horse shoe at the entrance to one's home, or carrying a rabbit's foot, wearing a "lucky shirt" or tying a string on one's wrist or neck for protection. And you'll find that such a person, if he did not wear it or were you to cut it off of him, he becomes afraid or doesn't feel comfortable, fearing that something will happen to him – which proves that this is from *shirk*. So if a person believes that these things can bring about benefit or protect him from harm, then he believes that these things have more power and more effect than Allaah's *Qadr* (Pre-decree), which is from Allaah's Actions! Here is where *shirk* enters and here is where the danger lies for our children, for these affairs can more easily enter upon them than sacrificing for other than Allaah and the like. For this we see that *Imaam* Muhammad bin 'Abdul-Wahhaab brought chapters related to all of these things in his *Kitaabut-Tawheed*. Let the reader refer to it and the explanations of the scholars, like *Fathul-Majeed* and those of *Shaykh* Ibn Baaz and *Shaykh* Ibn 'Uthaymeen, *Shaykh* 'Ubayd al-Jaabiree and other than them. {Translator}

[10] See *Majmoo' al-Fataawaa* of *Shaykhul-Islaam* Ibn Taymiyyah [10/149] {Translator}

[11] Al-Jinn (72):18

And the proof that calling upon other than Allaah is *kufr* (disbelief), is as He said, the Most High:

$$\text{وَمَن يَدْعُ مَعَ ٱللَّهِ إِلَٰهًا ءَاخَرَ لَا بُرْهَٰنَ لَهُۥ بِهِۦ فَإِنَّمَا حِسَابُهُۥ عِندَ رَبِّهِۦٓ إِنَّهُۥ لَا يُفْلِحُ ٱلْكَٰفِرُونَ}$$

"And whoever invokes (or worships), besides Allaah, any other *ilaah* (object of worship), of whom he has no proof for, then his reckoning is only with his Lord. Surely! *Al-Kaafiroon* (the disbelievers) will never be successful." [12]

And that is because *Du'aa* is from the greatest types of worship, as your Lord has said:

$$\text{وَقَالَ رَبُّكُمُ ٱدْعُونِىٓ أَسْتَجِبْ لَكُمْ إِنَّ ٱلَّذِينَ يَسْتَكْبِرُونَ عَنْ عِبَادَتِى سَيَدْخُلُونَ جَهَنَّمَ دَاخِرِينَ}$$

"Invoke Me (Alone, and ask Me for anything) I will respond to your (invocation). Verily! Those who scorn My worship [i.e. do not invoke Me, and do not believe in My Oneness] they will surely enter Hell in humiliation!" [13]

---

[12] Al-Mu'minoon (23):117
[13] Ghaafir (40):60

And the Messenger of Allaah (ﷺ) said in the *Sunan*: ((*Ad-Du'aa is worship*)) [14]

And the first and foremost of what Allaah made obligatory upon His servants is disbelief in the *taaghoot* (all false objects of worship) and *eemaan* (correct belief) in Allaah. He said, the Most High:

$$\text{وَلَقَدْ بَعَثْنَا فِى كُلِّ أُمَّةٍ رَّسُولًا أَنِ ٱعْبُدُوا۟ ٱللَّهَ وَٱجْتَنِبُوا۟ ٱلطَّٰغُوتَ}$$

"And verily, We have sent among every *Ummah* (community, nation) a Messenger (proclaiming): "Worship Allaah (Alone), and avoid (or keep away from) *Taaghoot* (all false deities that are worshipped besides Allaah)." [15]

And *at-Taaghoot* is: what is worshipped besides Allaah, and whoever is worshipped and he is pleased with that, like ash-Shaytaan, and the soothsayer and fortune-tellers, and the one

---

[14] *Al-Haafidh* Ibn Hajr said: It was collected by the Companions of the books of *Sunan* with a good (*jayyid*) chain of narration [*Fathul-Baaree*, in the chapter: *Bunyaa al-Islaam 'alaa khamis* (Islaam is built upon 5)]. It was collected by Aboo Daawood [#1479] and at-Tirmidhee [#3372] and declared authentic by *Shaykh* Al-Albaanee (refer to *Saheehul-Jaami'* [#3407]) and likewise *Shaykh* Muqbil bin Haadee al-Waadi'ee (*rahimahullaa*h) in *As-Saheehul-Musnad mimaa laysa fis-Saheehayn* in the *Musnad* of an-Nu'maan bin Basheer [vol.2: 9/1177].

[15] An-Nahl (16):36

who rules by other than what Allaah revealed [16], and every one who is followed (and) obeyed without right.

Al-'Allaamah Ibnul-Qayyim (رحمه الله تعالى): "*at-Taaghoot* comes from *at-taghyaan*, and it is going beyond the bounds and increasing upon them. Every created thing is a servant of Allaah, so if he goes beyond the bounds of this servitude, he becomes a *taaghoot*. So there is no worship except for Allaah, and no following except for the command of Allaah, and no obedience to the creation in disobedience to the Creator." [17]

---

[16] The *Shaykh* and *Imaam* 'Abdul-'Azeez bin Baaz (*rahimahullaah*) said: "Whoever makes permissible ruling by other than what Allaah revealed, or *zinaa* (fornication), or *ribaa* (taking interest), or other than them from those things that have been prohibited that are united upon in their being prohibited, then he has disbelieved with the major disbelief [that expels one from the Religion], and has transgressed with a major transgression, and has sinned with a major form of sinfulness. And whoever does them without declaring it to be permissible, then his disbelief is a minor disbelief [that does not expel one from the Religion], and his transgression is a minor form of transgression, and likewise his sinfulness." The transcribed speech of the *Shaykh* Ibn Baaz regarding the speech of *Shaykh* al-Albaanee in his book "*Fitnatut-Takfeer*".

[17] **Clarification:** The people of *Takfeer* (those who declare Muslims to be disbelievers due to sins) use certain words and terms from the *Deen* and interpret them according to their desires, contradicting what the Messenger (ﷺ) and his Companions were upon. And the Prophet (ﷺ) mentioned this in his saying: ***"The destruction of my Ummah is in the Book and the laban."*** And he explained what is meant by the Book: ***"(a people who) learn the Qur'aan and then explain it in a way which Allaah*** (ﷻ) ***did not send down."*** [*as-Saheehah* (6/647)] So they take the Qur'aan and explain it with their desires, and then declare the Muslim rulers and their deputies to be disbelievers, like we see in Algeria, 'Iraaq, Afghanistan and other Muslim countries. And then they shed the blood of the Muslims – rulers and the ruled – under the banner of *takfeer*. And this can be found in their books, like the book *Usool al-'Ilmiyyah feed-Da'watus-Salafiyyah* of 'Abdur-Rahmaan 'Abdul-Khaaliq who says: "Among these barriers (to the *da'wah*) is this mass apostasy that has engulfed the Muslim *Ummah*". And the examples like this are many. →

Question 5: So if it is said to you: what is your *Deen* (Religion)?

Answer: Then say: My *Deen* is Islaam. [18]

→ So the Prophet (ﷺ) mentioned that the destruction of his *Ummah* will come from these individuals who abandon the correct understanding of the Qur'aan, the understanding of the Prophet (ﷺ) and the Companions. Because of this you will find them saying that the Muslim Ruler of such and such country is a disbeliever, using their false understanding of the Qur'aan as proof for what they say. For example, they will say that some of the leaders of the GCC countries are disbelievers, or that the police or other government officials are disbelievers. And we have seen this in Kuwait and Saudi Arabia only recently! And the Messenger of Allaah (ﷺ) said: *"Indeed what I fear you the most is a man who reads the Qur'aan, until its joy and effects can be seen upon him, and he was a defensive support for Islaam, and he casts it off and throws it away behind his back, and he goes out (to attack) his neighbor with the sword and accuses him of shirk."* Hudhayfah (ﷺ) said: "I said: "O Prophet of Allaah! Which one of them is the first (has the most right) to be labeled with *shirk*, the accuser or the accused?" He said: *"The accuser."* [*As-Saheehah* (#3201) {Translator}

[18] Allaah said in His Book: **"Ibraaheem was neither a Jew nor a Christian, but he was a true muslim, a *Haneef* (one who is free from associating partners with Allaah in worship) and he was not of the *mushrikoon* (those who associate partners with Allaah in worship)."** [Aali –'Imraan (3):67] And the Messenger of Allaah (ﷺ) said: *"The Prophets are paternal brothers; their mothers are different, but their religion is one"*, meaning that the foundation of their religion is one, and it is *Tawheed*, even if they differ in the subsidiary matters and the prescribed laws.[al-Bukhaaree in the *Kitaabul-Anbiyyaa'*. See *Fath* (6/3328)] All of this shows that all of the Prophets and Messengers came with Islaam. As for what the people fell into after them, distorting the message that all of them were sent with, and then inventing new names for that, like "Christianity" and "Judaism", then this is nothing but innovation. Qataadah said: "By Allaah! Verily Judaism is a *bid'ah* (innovation), and verily Christianity is a *bid'ah*, and verily the *Hurooriyyah* (the Khawaarij) are a *bid'ah*, and verily the Sabians are a *bid'ah*. No book was sent down for them nor were they laid down as a way (*Sunnah*) to be followed by any prophet." [*Tafseerul-Qur'aan* of 'Abdur-Razzaaq (1/376) and its men are *thiqaat*] So that which Moosaa and 'Eesaa and all of the Prophets came with was Islaam. {Translator}

And the meaning of Islaam is: submission to Allaah with *Tawheed*, and compliance to Him by acting in obedience, and having love and allegiance towards the Muslims and enmity towards the people of *shirk* (the *Mushrikeen*). He, the Most High, said:

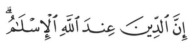

"Verily, the (only) religion with Allaah is Islaam." * ¹⁹

---

* **Benefit:** Allaah said: **"It is He (Allaah) Who has named you Muslims."** [al-Hajj (28):78] So according to what the *Imaam* mentions here – may Allaah have mercy upon him- it is not allowed for us to label Muslims with terms such as "liberal", "secularist" and the likes of that. In Islaam there is only Muslim, "*kaafir*" (disbeliever), "*munaafiq*" (a hypocrite, one who inwardly disbelieves while showing Islaam outwardly) or "*muslim faasiq*" (a disobedient, sinful Muslim) and the like of that. So if we want to make a judgment or a ruling upon a Muslim, we don't say "liberal" and other terms similar to this like the political groups do. Rather we make a ruling using the terms that Allaah has laid down in His legislation. Likewise we don't say that some of the Muslims are "*Islaamiyeen*" (Islaamists), because this term gives the indirect meaning that anyone who is not an "Islaamist" is not a Muslim. For example, we see in the newspapers that they often mention that there are "30 Islaamists in the parliament" of a particular Muslim country, and this gives the meaning that the rest of its members are not from the people of Islaam. And we fear that what is intended by this is *Takfeer* of the Muslims (declaring them to be disbelievers) who are not from their group. So these terms [i.e. liberal, secularist and Islaamist] are used by the people of the political groups and parties in the Muslim lands, giving the feeling that the *Deen* of Islaam is exclusively for their party and using the name of Islaam for the benefit of their group and its political gains to the exclusion of those who oppose them, when **"it is He (Allaah) Who has named you Muslims"**. *Shaykhul-Islaam* Ibn Taymiyyah said: "And Allaah the Most High indeed named us in the Qur'aan Muslims, believers, servants of Allaah. So we do not change the names that Allaah named us with for names invented by a people and their fathers that Allaah did not send down any authority for." [*Majmoo' al-Fataawaa* (3/415)] {Translator}

¹⁹ Aali-'Imraan (3):19

And He said:

$$\text{وَمَن يَبْتَغِ غَيْرَ الْإِسْلَٰمِ دِينًا فَلَن يُقْبَلَ مِنْهُ وَهُوَ فِي الْآخِرَةِ مِنَ الْخَاسِرِينَ}$$

"And whoever seeks a religion other than Islaam, it will never be accepted of him." [20] *

And it is authentically reported from the Prophet (ﷺ) that he said: *"Islaam is that you testify that Laa ilaaha illallaah and that Muhammad is the Messenger of Allaah, and to establish the Prayer, and pay the Zakaah, and to fast Ramadaan and to make the Pilgrimmage (Hajj) to the House if you are able to do so."* [21]*

And the meaning of *Laa ilaaha illallaah* is: there is nothing that has the right to be worshipped *in truth* except Allaah [22], as He said, the Most High:

---

[20] Aali-'Imraan (3):85

[21] From the famous *hadeeth* of Jibreel, collected by Muslim in *Kitaabul-Eemaan* (The Book of *Eemaan*) -Chapter: *Al-Eemaan wal-Islaam wal-Ihsaan*, #1 and 2] {Translator}

[22] This is the correct meaning of *Laa ilaaha illallaah*, as comes in the saying of Allaah (ﷻ): "That is because Allaah, He is the *Haqq* (Truth), and that which they call upon besides Him is *baatil* (false and futile)." [al-Hajj (22):62] So this *aayah* shows that there are gods that are worshipped besides Allaah, but all of them are worshipped in falsehood because none of them can bring about benefit or harm. Ibn Katheer said in his *tafseer* of this *aayah*: "Everything that is worshipped besides Him -the Most High- then it is false and futile because it does not have the ability to bring about harm or benefit." →

$$\text{وَإِذْ قَالَ إِبْرَاهِيمُ لِأَبِيهِ وَقَوْمِهِ إِنَّنِي بَرَآءٌ مِّمَّا تَعْبُدُونَ ﴿٢٦﴾ إِلَّا الَّذِي فَطَرَنِي فَإِنَّهُ سَيَهْدِينِ ﴿٢٧﴾ وَجَعَلَهَا كَلِمَةً بَاقِيَةً فِي عَقِبِهِ لَعَلَّهُمْ يَرْجِعُونَ}$$

"And (remember) when Ibraaheem said to his father and his people: 'Verily, I am innocent of what you worship, Except Him (i.e. I worship none but Allaah Alone) Who did create me, and verily, He will guide me.' And he made it [i.e. the statement *Laa ilaaha illallaah*] a lasting Word among his offspring, that they may turn back (i.e. to repent to Allaah or receive admonition)." 23

→ As for those who claim that *Laa ilaaha illallaah* means "there is no god but Allaah", then this saying opposes this *aayah*, as does the saying of those who claim it means "there is no creator" or "Law-giver except Allaah." All of these statements oppose the understanding of the *Salaf*.

So whoever puts a grave as an intermediary between himself and Allaah has committed *shirk* with Allaah. If one were to reflect over this statement they would find that all of the other religions have this type of *shirk*. The Jews go to the graves of their "*tzadikim*" and believe that they shield the world and that without their prayers the world would be destroyed. The Jews of the Chavrei Habakuk of Morocco visit the tomb of their prophet Habakuk. Some Christians believe that the graves of their saints can bring about miracles and healing, like the grave of Fatima in Portugal. The Shee'ah go to the Shrines of 'Alee, Hussayn and even Khomeini, while the Soofees go to the "*dargah*" (shrines) of the likes of al-Badawi, al-Jeelaanee, Jalaluddin Bukhari, Bahauddin Naqshaband and others. As for *Ahlus-Sunnah*, then they do not make *du'aa* to any grave, even the grave of Allaah's Messenger (ﷺ). And this shows the difference between *Ahlul-Haqq* and all of the other religions and sects. And this is from *al-Furqaan* (making the distinction between Truth and falsehood)! {Translator}

23 Az-Zukhruf (43):26-28

And the proof for the Prayer (*as-Salaah*) and *Zakaah* is His saying, the Most High:

$$\text{وَمَا أُمِرُوا إِلَّا لِيَعْبُدُوا اللَّهَ مُخْلِصِينَ لَهُ الدِّينَ حُنَفَاءَ وَيُقِيمُوا الصَّلَاةَ وَيُؤْتُوا الزَّكَاةَ وَذَلِكَ دِينُ الْقَيِّمَةِ}$$

"And they were commanded not, but that they should worship Allaah, and worship none but Him Alone (abstaining from ascribing partners to Him), and perform the *Salaah* and give *Zakaah*: and that is the right religion." [24]

So in this *aayah*, He began with *at-Tawheed* and being free and disavowing oneself from *shirk*. (So) the greatest thing that He ordered with is *at-Tawheed*, and the greatest thing that He prohibited is *shirk*. And He ordered (after that) with establishment of the *Salaah* and paying the *Zakaah*, and these are the foundational principles of the *Deen*, and what comes after it from the religious rites follows after it.

And the proof for the obligation of Fasting (*as-Siyaam*) is His saying, the Most High:

$$\text{يَا أَيُّهَا الَّذِينَ آمَنُوا كُتِبَ عَلَيْكُمُ الصِّيَامُ كَمَا كُتِبَ عَلَى الَّذِينَ مِن قَبْلِكُمْ}$$

---

[24] al-Bayyinah (98):5

"O you who believe! Fasting has been prescribed for you just as it was prescribed for those before you…"

To his saying:

شَهْرُ رَمَضَانَ ٱلَّذِىٓ أُنزِلَ فِيهِ ٱلْقُرْءَانُ هُدًى لِّلنَّاسِ وَبَيِّنَـٰتٍ مِّنَ ٱلْهُدَىٰ وَٱلْفُرْقَانِ ۚ فَمَن شَهِدَ مِنكُمُ ٱلشَّهْرَ فَلْيَصُمْهُ

"The month of Ramadaan in which was revealed the Qur'aan, a guidance for mankind and clear proofs for the guidance and *al-Furqaan* (the distinction between Truth and falsehood)[25]. So

---

[25] **Benefit:** *al-Furqaan* (distinguishing between Truth and falsehood) is the foundation of the *Deen*. And *al-Furqaan* is the name of the Qur'aan and is from the names of the Prophet (ﷺ), for he is "*al-Faariq*". And indeed Allaah sent every Prophet and every Messenger with *al-Furqaan*, to clarify for their peoples Truth from falsehood. Allaah said: **"And (remember) when We gave Moosaa the book and *al-Furqaan* so that you may be guided aright."** [al-Baqarah (2):53] And He said: **"Blessed be He Who sent down *al-Furqaan* to His slave** (Muhammad ﷺ) **that he may be a warner to the *'Aalameen* (mankind and jinns)."** [Al-Furqaan (25):1] So it is from the characteristics of *Ahlus-Sunnah* to strive for this distinction between Truth and falsehood in order to distinguish and separate the methodology of *Ahlul-Haqq* (the people of the Truth) from the deviated methodologies and false statements of the people of innovation. And this was the way of the Messenger (ﷺ) and the way of his Companions. So whoever is closest in adhering to what the Companions of the Messenger (ﷺ) were upon is the closest to *Furqaan*. And whoever is farthest from following their way is the farthest from *Furqaan*. And the one who teaches the people and does not distinguish Truth from falsehood for them, and speaks regarding the *Deen* of →

whoever of you witnesses the month (of Ramadaan)[i.e. is present in his land and healthy enough to fast] then he must fast it." [26]

And the proof for the obligation of the Hajj is His saying, the Most High:

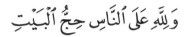

"And Hajj (pilgrimage to Makkah) to the House (Ka'bah) is a duty that mankind owes to Allaah" [27]

And the Usool (fundamental principles) of Eemaan are six: that you believe in Allaah, and it is *eemaan* in His Existence, His *Ruboobiyyah* (Lordship), His *Uloohiyyah* (His sole right to be worshipped) and His *Asmaa' was-Sifaat* (Beautiful Names and Perfect Attributes); His Angels; His divinely-revealed Books; His *Rusul* (Messengers); the Last Day, and *al-Qadar*,

---

→ Allaah in generalities and conceals the Truth that he knows, then he is someone who is cheating the people, because he is not giving them *Furqaan* as the Prophet (ﷺ) and his Companions did. {Translator}

[26] Al-Baqarah (2):183-185
[27] Aali-'Imraan (3):97

the good of it and the bad of it [28]. And the *daleel* (proof) is what is in the *Saheeh* from the *hadeeth* of 'Umar bin al-Khattaab ﷺ. He said: "One day while we were sitting with the Messenger of Allaah (ﷺ) there appeared before us a man whose clothes were exceedingly white and whose hair was exceedingly black; no signs of journey were to be seen on him..." to his saying : "Tell me about *Eemaan*."
He (the Prophet) said: ***"It is to believe in Allaah, His Angels, His Books, His Messengers, and the Last Day, and to believe in Al-Qadr (the Pre-Decree), both the good and the bad of it"***, (to the end of) the *hadeeth*. It was collected by al-Bukhaaree and Muslim.

Question 6: If it is said to you: Who is your prophet?

Answer: Then say: Our prophet is Muhammad bin 'Abdullaah bin 'Abdul-Muttalib bin Haashim bin 'Abd Manaaf (ﷺ).

Allaah the Most High chose him from Quraysh, and they are the best and most elite of the Arabs, the offspring of Ismaa'eel. And He sent him to *al-ahmar* (the red) and *al-aswad*

---

[28] Everything has been written by Allaah whether good or bad. If someone from one's family dies for example, he remembers that the fruit of *Eemaan* is *Tasleem* (total submission) to what Allaah decreed. If someone has an accident, lost his job, becomes sick or is afflicted with Cancer or any other disease, it is from *Eemaan* to believe that all of this is from Allaah's *Qadar*, its good and its bad, and that Allaah decreed this for a wisdom. So the Muslim must be content and submit himself to what Allaah has decreed and commanded if he truly believes in *al-Qadar*. And if he is afflicted with something in regards to his health, wealth or his family, he says **"Inna lillaahi wa inna ilayhi raaji'oon"** ("Verily to Allaah we belong and verily to Him we shall return.") [al-Baqarah (2):156] {Translator}

(the black) [29], and sent down upon him the Book and the *Hikmah* [30]. So he called the people to making worship sincerely and purely for Allaah and abandoning what they used to worship besides Allaah, from idols, stones, trees, Prophets and the righteous, Angels and other than that. So he called the people to abandon *shirk* and he fought them so that they may abandon it and that they single out Allaah in worship, Alone without any partner, as He said, the Most High:

---

[29] Our *Shaykh* Ṭaariq as-Subay'ee – may Allaah preserve him- explained that this term means: "to all of the various types of peoples." What the *Shaykh* mentions comes from the *hadeeth* collected by *Imaam* Muslim in his *Saheeh* [#521] that the Messenger of Allaah (ﷺ) said: *"I have been given five that were not given to anyone before me: Every prophet was sent to his people specifically, and I was sent to all, ahmar (red) and aswad (black)..."* An-Nawawee explains: "What is intended by *al-Ahmar* is the white from the '*ajm* (non-Arabs) and other than them. And by the *al-Aswad*, the Arabs, due to the predominance of brownness in them and other than them from those that are dark-skinned." And he goes on to mention: "And it is said: *Al-Ahmar*, the human beings, and *al-Aswad*, the Jinn. And all of them are correct for indeed he was sent to all of them." [*Sharh Saheeh* Muslim (5/521), *Kitaab al-Masaajid*] {Translator}

[30] The scholars of *Tafseer* explain that the *Hikmah* is the Sunnah of Allaah's Messenger (ﷺ). *Imaam* Ibn Jareer aṭ-Ṭabaree [d.310H] – *rahimahullaah* – said regarding the saying of Allaah, the Most High: **"Similarly We have sent among you a Messenger (Muhammad) of your own, reciting to you Our Verses (the Qur'aan) and sanctifying you, and teaching you the Book (the Qur'aan) and the *Hikmah*..."** [al-Baqarah (2):151]: "and He (Allaah) means by the *Hikmah* the *Sunan*, and understanding of the Religion." And *al-Haafith* Ibn Katheer said regarding this verse: "And he teaches them the Book, and it is the Qur'aan, and the *Hikmah*, and it is the Sunnah." Likewise, the Messenger of Allaah (ﷺ) said: *"Indeed I was sent with the Book (the Qur'aan) and what is like it along with it..."* [*Sunan Abee Daawood*: (#4604): Declared *saheeh* by *Shaykh* al-Albaanee] And all of this shows that the Sunnah, like the Qur'aan, is revelation from Allaah. Ḥassaan bin 'Aṭiyyah said: "Jibreel used to descend upon the Messenger of Allaah (ﷺ) with the Sunnah just like he descended upon him with the Qur'aan, and would teach it to him just as he used to teach him the Qur'aan." [*As-Sunnah* of al-Marwazee (104)] {Translator}

$$\text{قُلْ إِنَّمَا أَدْعُواْ رَبِّي وَلَا أُشْرِكُ بِهِ أَحَدًا}$$

"Say (O Muḥammad): "I invoke only my Lord (Allaah Alone), and I associate none as partners along with Him." [31]

And He said, the Most High:

$$\text{قُلِ ٱللَّهَ أَعْبُدُ مُخْلِصًا لَّهُ دِينِي}$$

"Say (O Muḥammad): Allaah Alone I worship by doing religious deeds sincerely for His sake only and not to show-off, and not to set up rivals with Him in worship." [32]

And He said, the Most High:

$$\text{قُلْ إِنَّمَا أُمِرْتُ أَنْ أَعْبُدَ ٱللَّهَ وَلَا أُشْرِكَ بِهِ إِلَيْهِ أَدْعُواْ وَإِلَيْهِ مَـَٔابِ}$$

"Say (O Muḥammad): "I am commanded only to worship Allaah (Alone) and not to join partners with Him. To Him (Alone) I call and to Him is my return." [33]

---

[31] al-Jinn (72):20
[32] az-Zumar (39):14
[33] Ar-Ra'd (13):36

And He said, the Most High:

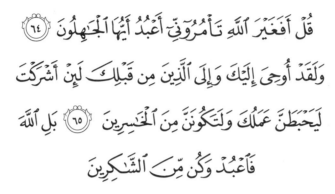

"Say (O Muḥammad to the polytheists, etc.): "Do you order me to worship other than Allaah O you fools?" And indeed it has been revealed to you (O Muḥammad), as it was to those (Allaah's Messengers) before you: "If you join others in worship with Allaah, (then) surely (all) your deeds will be in vain, and you will certainly be among the losers." Nay! But worship Allaah (Alone and none else), and be among the grateful." [34]

And from the *Uṣool* (foundations) of *Eemaan*, which saves from *kufr* (disbelief) are: Belief in the Resurrection, Retribution and Reckoning, and *Jannah* (Paradise) and the Hellfire are real.

And He said, the Most High:

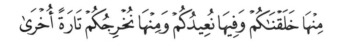

---

[34] Az-Zumar (39):64-66

> "Thereof (the earth) We created you, and into it We shall return you, and from it We shall bring you out once again." [35]

And He said, the Most High:

$$\text{وَإِن تَعْجَبْ فَعَجَبٌ قَوْلُهُمْ أَءِذَا كُنَّا تُرَٰبًا أَءِنَّا لَفِى خَلْقٍ جَدِيدٍ ۗ أُو۟لَٰٓئِكَ ٱلَّذِينَ كَفَرُوا۟ بِرَبِّهِمْ ۖ وَأُو۟لَٰٓئِكَ ٱلْأَغْلَٰلُ فِىٓ أَعْنَاقِهِمْ ۖ وَأُو۟لَٰٓئِكَ أَصْحَٰبُ ٱلنَّارِ ۖ هُمْ فِيهَا خَٰلِدُونَ}$$

> "And if you (O Muḥammad) wonder (at these polytheists who deny your message of Islaamic Monotheism and have taken besides Allaah others for worship who can neither harm nor benefit), then wondrous is their saying: "When we are dust, shall we indeed then be (raised) in a new creation?" They are those who disbelieve in their Lord! They are those who will have iron chains tying their hands to their necks. They will be dwellers of the Fire to abide therein." [36]

And in this *aayah* is a proof that whoever rejects the Resurrection has disbelieved with a *kufr* that makes abiding eternally in the Hellfire obligatory. May Allaah grant us protection from *kufr* and the actions of *kufr*.

---

[35] ṬaaHaa (20):55
[36] Ar-Ra'd (13):5

So these *aayaat* contain a clarification of what He sent the Prophet (صلى الله عليه و على آله و سلم) with, from making worship sincerely for Allaah, and the prohibition of worshipping anything besides Allaah and restricting worship to His worship. And this is His *Deen* that he called the people to, and strove against them due to it, as He said, the Most High:

وَقَٰتِلُوهُمْ حَتَّىٰ لَا تَكُونَ فِتْنَةٌ وَيَكُونَ ٱلدِّينُ كُلُّهُۥ لِلَّهِ فَإِنِ ٱنتَهَوْاْ فَإِنَّ ٱللَّهَ بِمَا يَعْمَلُونَ بَصِيرٌ

"And fight them until there is no more *Fitnah* (disbelief and polytheism: i.e. worshipping others besides Allaah) and the religion (worship) will all be for Allaah Alone." [37]

And indeed Allaah the Most High sent him (as a Messenger) at forty years of age, so he called the people to *al-Ikhlaas* (making worship solely and sincerely for Him) and abandoning the worship of what is besides Allaah, for a

---

[37] Al-Anfaal (8):39

period of thirteen years [38]. Then he was taken up to the heavens and the five daily prayers were made obligatory upon him – without any intermediary between him and Allaah the Most High in that. [39]

Then He commanded him after that with the *Hijrah* (migration), so he emigrated to al-Madeenah and was ordered with *Jihaad*. So he strove in *Jihaad* for the sake of Allaah, a true striving, for nearly ten years until the people entered into the *Deen* of Allaah in droves. So when he had completed sixty-three years – and all praise and thanks are due to Allaah – the *Deen* was perfected and the favor was completed and the trust and message from Allaah was conveyed. Then Allaah the Most High took him (by death)– صلوات الله و سلامه عليه. [40]

---

[38] Whoever calls the people to the Truth must be patient. Allaah said: **"So bear patiently (O Mu<u>h</u>ammad) what they say, and glorify the praises of your Lord before the rising of the sun, and before its setting, and during some of the hours of the night, and at the sides of the day, that you may become pleased with the reward which Allaah will give you."** [<u>T</u>aa-Haa (20):130] So we find that the Prophet (ﷺ) was patient, kind and gentle in calling the people to the *Deen* of Allaah. Allaah mentions: **"And by the Mercy of Allaah, you dealt with them gently. And had you been severe and harsh hearted (towards them), they would have broken away from around you…"** [Aali 'Imraan (3):159] And the *da'wah* that the Prophet (ﷺ) and the Companions were upon is built and established upon *Sabr* (patience): **"They will not be harmed by those who forsake them (in the time of aiding the <u>H</u>aqq) nor those who oppose them up to the Command of Allaah comes and they are manifest to the people."** [declared *sa<u>h</u>eeh* by *Shaykh* al-Albaanee. See *Sa<u>h</u>ee<u>h</u>ul-Jaami'* (#7290)] {Translator}

[39] This was during the *Mi'raaj* (Ascension) of the Prophet (ﷺ) as comes in the long *<u>h</u>adeeth* of Maalik bin <u>S</u>a'<u>s</u>a'ah, collected by al-Bu<u>kh</u>aaree in his *<u>S</u>a<u>h</u>eeh* in *Kitaab Fa<u>d</u>aa'il A<u>sh</u>aabin-Nabee* (The Book of the Merits of the Companions of the Prophet) in the chapter *Al-Mi'raaj*. {Translator}

[40] In one wording of the text it is written "the *Deen* was completed, and he conveyed the news from that which Allaah the Most High had informed him of his death…."

And the first of the Messengers was Nooh (Noah- ﷺ) [41] and the last of them was Muḥammad (ﷺ), just as He said, the Most High:

$$\text{إِنَّا أَوْحَيْنَا إِلَيْكَ كَمَا أَوْحَيْنَا إِلَىٰ نُوحٍ وَالنَّبِيِّينَ مِنْ بَعْدِهِ}$$

"Verily, We have inspired you (O Muḥammad) as We inspired Nooh and the Prophets after him." [42]

---

[41] **Benefit:** Ibn 'Abbaas (رضي الله عنه) said: "There was between Nooh and Aadam ten generations, all of them upon a legislated way from the Truth. Then they differed, so Allaah sent the Prophets as bringers of glad tidings and warners." [aṭ-Ṭabaree in his *tafseer* (4/275) and al-Ḥaakim (2/546) who said: "It is authentic according to the criterion of al-Bukhaaree." Adh-Dhahabee also agreed]. And al-Ḥaafidh Ibn Katheer said: "And the first statement from Ibn 'Abbaas is more authentic in its chain of narration and meaning, because the people were upon the *millah* (religion) of Aadam until they began worshipping the idols. So Allaah sent Nooh (عليه السلام) to them, and he was the first messenger sent by Allaah to the people of the earth." [*Tafseer Ibn Katheer* in explanation of *aayah* 213 of Sooratul-Baqarah]. It is also related from Ibn 'Abbaas that he said: "Indeed these five names were (the names) of righteous men from the people of Nooh. When they died Shayṭaan whispered to their people that they should make statues of them and to place these statues in their places of gathering as a reminder of them, and to name them with their names, so they did it. So none from amongst them worshipped these statues, until when they died and the knowledge (of the purpose of the statues) was forgotten. Then (the next generation) began to worship them." [al-Bukhaaree in *Kitaabut-Tafseer*] So from this we see how *shirk* entered upon the people after all of them had been people of *Tawḥeed*, through going to extremes regarding the people of piety and righteousness. And we see that Nooh (عليه السلام) was the first messenger sent to them by Allaah. See *Tahdheerus-Saajid min Ittikhaadhil-Quboori Masaajid* of *Shaykh* al-Albaanee (pp.135-140). {Translator}

[42] An-Nisaa' (4):163

And He said, the Most High:

$$وَمَا مُحَمَّدٌ إِلَّا رَسُولٌ$$

"Mu<u>h</u>ammad (ﷺ) is no more than
a Messenger." [43]

$$مَّا كَانَ مُحَمَّدٌ أَبَآ أَحَدٍ مِّن رِّجَالِكُمْ وَلَٰكِن رَّسُولَ ٱللَّهِ وَخَاتَمَ ٱلنَّبِيِّـۧنَ ۗ وَكَانَ ٱللَّهُ بِكُلِّ شَىْءٍ عَلِيمًا ﴿٤٠﴾$$

"Mu<u>h</u>ammad (ﷺ) is not the father of any man amongst you, but he is the Messenger of Allaah and the last of the Prophets. And Allaah is Ever All-Aware of everything." [44]

---

[43] Aali -'Imran (3):144
[44] Al-A<u>h</u>zaab (33):40

And the best of the Messengers is our Prophet Muhammad (صلى الله عليه وعلى آله وسلم). And the best of mankind after the Prophets (صلى الله عليه وسلم) is Aboo Bakr (رضي الله عنه), and 'Umar (رضي الله عنه), and 'Uthmaan (رضي الله عنه) and 'Alee (رضي الله عنه)– may Allaah be pleased with all of the Companions and the Wives of the Prophet (ﷺ), the Mothers of the Believers, and his fine, pure family. The Messenger of Allaah (ﷺ) said (that) the best of generations "*is my generation, then those who follow them, then those who follow them.*" [45]

And 'Eesaa (Jesus- ﷺ) will descend from the heavens and slay the Dajjaal [46].

---

[45] Collected by al-Bukhaaree and Muslim with the wording: **"The best of people are my generation, then those that follow them, then those that follow them."** And in another wording collected by Muslim: **"The best of my Ummah is the generation that I was sent in, then those that follow them, then those that follow them."** [refer to *as-Saheehah* of *Shaykh* al-Albaanee(#699-700)]

Shaykhul-Islaam Ibn Taymiyyah [d.728H] said: "the *Deen* of Allaah is only that which he sent His Messengers with, and sent down His Books with, and it is the Straight Path, and it is the way of the Companions of Allaah's Messenger (ﷺ), the best of *Qaroon* (generations), and the best of the *Ummah*, and most noble of the creation with Allaah after the Prophets." [*at-Tadmuriyyah* pg.236, Maktabah al-'Ubaykaan] So this shows us that the correct way to understand the Religion is through the understanding of the Companions and those who followed them from the first three noble generations. So we understand the Qur'aan and Sunnah according to how they understood the Qur'aan and Sunnah. And the proofs to show this reality are many. {Translator}

[46] There are more than forty authentic narrations from the Prophet (ﷺ) regarding the coming out of the Dajjaal (the false messiah) and the descending of Prophet 'Eesaa (ﷺ). The Messenger of Allaah (ﷺ) described that he will be of flesh and blood, appearing from between Shaam (the area around present-day Syria) and 'Iraaq, "*kaafir*" will be written between his eyes, and one of his eyes will be like a floating grape. He will cause great tribulations and mischief in the earth. 'Eesaa, the son of Mary (عليها السلام) will descend and slay him at the gate of Al-Ludd. Refer to *Qisatul-Maseehid-Dajjaal wa nuzool 'Eesaa 'alayhis-Salaatu was-salaam* of *Shaykh* al-Albaanee. {Translator}

And all praise and thanks are due to Allaah."

End of this Treatise

Examples from the Qur'aan, the Authentic Sunnah and Statements of the Salaf Related to raising Children

Compiled and Prepared by
Aboo Sufyaan 'Uthmaan Beecher

Reviewed by
Shaykh Aboo 'Uthmaan Muhammad al-'Anjaree

A Comfort for the Eyes

1 - Ibn 'Abbaas (رضي الله عنهما) said regarding the saying of Allaah (عز وجل):

وَٱلَّذِينَ يَقُولُونَ رَبَّنَا هَبْ لَنَا مِنْ أَزْوَٰجِنَا وَذُرِّيَّٰتِنَا قُرَّةَ أَعْيُنٍ وَٱجْعَلْنَا لِلْمُتَّقِينَ إِمَامًا ۷٤

"And those who say: "Our Lord! Bestow on us from our wives and our offspring who will be the comfort of our eyes, and make us leaders and guides for the pious." [47]

"They mean: who will act in obedience towards You, so by them our eyes will become comforted in the *dunyaa* (the life of this world) and the *Aakhirah* (the Hereafter)." [48]

2 - <u>H</u>azm said: I heard Katheer ask al-<u>H</u>asan (al-Ba<u>s</u>ree): "O Aboo Sa'eed! Allaah's saying:

وَٱلَّذِينَ يَقُولُونَ رَبَّنَا هَبْ لَنَا مِنْ أَزْوَٰجِنَا وَذُرِّيَّٰتِنَا قُرَّةَ

"And those who say: "Our Lord! Bestow on us from our wives and our offspring who will be the comfort of our eyes…"

---

[47] Al-Furqaan (25):74
[48] See *Tafseer a<u>t</u>-<u>T</u>abaree*

"In the *dunyaa* or *Aakhirah*?" He said: "No, rather in the *dunyaa*." He said: "And what is that?" He said: "The believer sees his wife and his child acting in obedience to Allaah (ﷻ)." [49]

3 – And ad-Dahhaak said regarding this *aayah* (verse): "They say: 'Make our wives and our offspring people of righteousness and *taqwaa*.'" [50]

4 - 'Amru bin Murrah said: "I asked Sa'eed bin Jubayr about His saying – the Most High:

$$\text{وَٱلَّذِينَ ءَامَنُوا۟ وَٱتَّبَعَتْهُمْ ذُرِّيَّتُهُم بِإِيمَٰنٍ أَلْحَقْنَا بِهِمْ ذُرِّيَّتَهُمْ}$$

"And those who believe and whose offspring follow them in *Eemaan*, We will join their offspring with them…" [51]

He said: "Ibn 'Abbaas said: 'The believer, his offspring will be raised up for him (to join him), even if they were less then him in deeds, so Allaah (ﷻ) will make them a comfort for his eyes.'" [52]

---

[49] *Al-Imaam* at-Tabaree in his *tafseer*, *Kitaabul-'Iyaal* of *al-Imaam*, *al-Haafidh* Ibn Abeed-Dunyaa (#435)
[50] *Kitaabul-'Iyaal* (#428)
[51] At-Toor (52):21
[52] Collected by at-Tabaree in his *tafseer* and by Ibn Abeed-Dunyaa in *Kitaabul-'Iyaal* (#361)

Giving the Children a Good Beginning

5 – Aboo Hurayrah (ﷻ) reported that the Messenger of Allaah (ﷺ) said: *"A woman is married for four: for her wealth, her position (or social status), her beauty and her deen (religion) – so choose the woman who possesses (good) religion, may your hands be covered in dust (if you don't)."* [53]

> ❁ *Al-Haafidh* Ibn Hajr said: "And the meaning is that the correctness and suitability of the woman who possesses good religion and honor is so that the *Deen* be the end goal of his thinking in everything, especially in regards to what will accompany him for a long time. So the Prophet (ﷺ) ordered him to get the woman of *Deen* which is the highest of all aspirations." [54]

6 - Ibn 'Abbaas (رضي الله عنهما) narrated that the Prophet (ﷺ) said: *"If one of you says when he comes to his wife for sexual intercourse:*

بِاسْمِ اللَّهِ اللَّهُمَّ جَنِّبْنِي الشَّيْطَانَ وَجَنِّبْ الشَّيْطَانَ مَا رَزَقْتَنَا

In the name of Allaah, O Allaah, protect me from shaytaan and protect what You bestow upon us [i.e. a

---

[53] Al-Bukhaaree in *Kitaabun-Nikaah* (The Book of Marriage)-Chapter: "Choosing (the woman) for *Deen*" and Muslim in the chapter "The Desirability of marrying one who possesses *deen*", Aboo Daawood (#2047), an-Nasaa'ee (#3230), Ibn Maajah (#1858), and al-Bayhaqee (#13751).

[54] see *al-Fath* (9/4902)

child] from shayṭaan), then that is decreed for them, or a child is decreed for them, shayṭaan will never harm him." ⁵⁵

❈ *Al-Ḥaafidh* Ibn Ḥajr said: "And his saying **"shayṭaan will never harm him"**, meaning: he will not harm the child for whom it (the *du'aa*) is mentioned for, by way of him having the ability to cause harm to him in his *Deen* or his body. The meaning is not the removal of the whisperings (of shayṭaan) from their origin." ⁵⁶

7 – 'Abdullaah bin 'Aamir al-Yaḥsabee (﷠) narrated that the Messenger of Allaah (ﷺ) said: ***"The best of names are 'Abdullaah and 'Abdur-Raḥmaan, and the most truthful of names are Hamaam and Ḥaarith, and the most evil of names are Ḥarb and Murrah."*** ⁵⁷

8 – Aboo Hurayrah, Jaabir bin 'Abdillaah and Anas (رضي الله عنهم) all reported that the Messenger of Allaah (ﷺ) said: ***"Name***

---

⁵⁵ Al-Bukhaaree in *Kitaabud-Da'waat* (Book of Supplications) and *Kitaabun-Nikaaḥ* (The Book of Marriage) - Chapter: "What a man says when he comes to his family (for intercourse)", Muslim in *Kitaabun-Nikaaḥ*, Chapter: "What is recommended to say at the time of intercourse". The transliteration of the *du'aa* is as follows: **Bismillaah, Allaahumma jannibneesh-shayṭaan, wa jannibash-shayṭaan maa razaqtanaa**

⁵⁶ *Fatḥul-Baree* (11/6164)

⁵⁷ At-Tirmidhee (#2833 and 2834), Ibn Maajah (#3728), Aboo Daawood (#4949), *al-Irwaa'* (#1176), *Ṣaḥeeḥul-Kalimiṭ-Ṭayyib* (pg. 77). *Shaykh* al-Albaanee said: "And this chain is *mursal ṣaḥeeḥ*, all of its men are trustworthy narrators." See *Aṣ-Ṣaḥeeḥah* (#904 & 1040)

with my name [Mu<u>h</u>ammad] ***and do not give my kunyah*** [Abool-Qaasim]***.***" ⁵⁸

9 - Samurah (☺) narrated that the Messenger of Allaah (☺) said: ***"The young boy (ghulaam) is in pledge for his 'aqeeqah. He is sacrificed for on the seventh day, and he is named and his head shaved."*** ⁵⁹

10 - It was reported by Daawood bin Qays, from 'Amru bin Shu'ayb from his father, from his grandfather that the Messenger of Allaah (☺) was asked about the *'Aqeeqah*, so he

---

⁵⁸ Al-Bu<u>kh</u>aaree in *Kitaabul-Adab* (The Book of Manners) -Chapter: The saying of the Prophet (☺): *"Name with my name and do not give my kunyah"* and *Kitaabul-Anbiyyaa'* (The Book of the Prophets) -Chapter: "The *kunyah* of the Prophet (☺)", Muslim in *Kitaabul-Adab* (The Book of Manners) - Chapter: "The prohibition of giving the *kunyah* Abool-Qaasim", Aboo Daawood (#4965) and A<u>h</u>mad in his *Musnad*. The Salaf have differed in this issue. *Shay<u>kh</u>ul-Islaam* Ibnul-Qayyim discusses these differences of opinion and breaks them down into four sayings amongst the Salaf: (1) that it is not allowed to use the *kunyah* of the Prophet (☺) absolutely, whether it is coupled with his name or by itself, (2) the prohibition is in regards to using his name and his *kunyah* together, (3) it is allowed to use them both together, the prohibition being abrogated, and (4) the prohibition of giving the *kunyah* Abool-Qaasim was specific to the Prophet's lifetime, and after his death (☺) it is allowed. After mentioning the proofs for each opinion, Ibnul-Qayyim says: "And what is correct is that naming with his name is permissible, and giving his *kunyah* is prohibited, and the prohibition during his lifetime is more severe, and combining the two is prohibited." Refer to *Zaadul-Ma'aad* (2/314-317, Publ. Ar-Risaalah).

⁵⁹ At-Tirmi<u>dh</u>ee (#1522), Ibn Maajah (#3165) and others, and declared *<u>s</u>a<u>h</u>ee<u>h</u>* by *Shay<u>kh</u>* al-Albaanee in *<u>S</u>a<u>h</u>eehul-Jaami'* (#4184) and *al-Irwaa'* (#1165).
Benefit: *al-<u>H</u>aafi<u>dh</u>* Ibn 'Abdil-Barr mentions in his *al-Isti<u>dh</u>kaar* (4/316): "And ash-Shaafi'ee, A<u>h</u>mad, Is<u>h</u>aaq, Aboo Thawr and a<u>t</u>-<u>T</u>abaraanee said: The *'Aqeeqah* is a *sunnah*; it is obligatory to do it and it should not be abandoned for the one who has the ability to do it."
As for shaving the head, *Ash-Shay<u>kh</u>* Ibn Baaz said in his *Fataawaa* (10/48): "The *Sunnah* is to shave the head of the boy when naming him on the seventh day only. As for the female then her head is not shaved."

said: *"Whoever loves that he sacrifice for his child then let him do so. For a boy, two sheep of equal age, and for a girl a sheep."* [60]

---

[60] Aboo Daawood (#2842), an-Nasaa'ee (#4215-6), al-Haakim (4/238) and others. See *As-Saheehah* (#1655).

Establishing a conducive environment for Children in the home

11 – 'Aa'ishah reported that the Messenger of Allaah (ﷺ) said: *"If Allaah wants goodness for a household He enters upon them ar-Rifq (gentleness and kindness)."* [61]

12 - Aboo Moosaa (ؓ) narrated that the Prophet (ﷺ) said: *"The example of the home in which Allaah is made mention of and the home in which Allaah is not made mention of is like the example of the living and the dead."* [62]

13 – Aboo Hurayrah (ؓ) reported that the Messenger of Allaah (ﷺ) said: *"Do not make your homes like graveyards, indeed Shaytaan avoids the home in which Sooratul-Baqarah is read."* [63]

14 – Hafs bin Ghayaath al-Hanafee narrated that Aboo Hurayrah (ؓ) said: "Indeed the home becomes spacious for its inhabitants, and the *Malaa'ikah* visit it and the *shayaateen* abandon it, and its goodness is increased if the Qur'aan is recited in it. And indeed the home becomes narrow and restricted upon its inhabitants, and the *Malaa'ikah* abandon it

---

[61] *Shu'abul-Eemaan* of al-Bayhaqee. Declared *saheeh* by *Shaykh* al-Albaanee in *Saheehul-Jaami'* (#303), *Al-Mishkaat* (#3707).

[62] Muslim in *Kitaabu Salaatil-Musaafireen* (The Book of the Prayer of the Traveller) -Chapter: "the recommendation of voluntary prayers in one's home".

[63] Muslim in *Kitaabu Salaatil-Musaafireen* - Chapter: "the recommendation of voluntary prayers in one's home", at-Tirmidhee (#2877) and *Ahkaamul-Janaa'iz* of *Shaykh* al-Albaanee (pg. 212)

and the *shayaateen* visit it, and its goodness is decreased if the Qur'aan is not recited in it." [64]

---

[64] Ad-Daarimee (4/3310), *mawqoof* on Aboo Hurayrah.

Showing Love, Affection and Mercy towards the Children

15 - Aboo Hurayrah (﷽) said: "Allaah's Messenger (ﷺ) kissed Hasan bin 'Alee, and Al-Aqra'a bin Haabis at-Tameemee was sitting with him, so Al-Aqra'a said: 'Verily I have ten sons, (and) I never kissed any one of them.' So the Messenger of Allaah (ﷺ) looked at him, then he said: ***"Whoever does not show mercy will not be shown mercy."*** [65]

16 - 'Aa'ishah (﷽) narrated that a Bedouin man came to the Prophet (ﷺ), and he said: "Do you kiss the children? We don't kiss them!" The Prophet (ﷺ) said: ***"I cannot put mercy in your heart after Allaah has taken it away from it."*** [66]

17 - Aboo 'Uthmaan reported that 'Umar (﷽) hired a man, so the employee said: 'Verily I have such and such number of sons, (and) I did not kiss (even) one from amongst them!' So 'Umar contended, or he said: "Verily Allaah (ﷻ) does not have mercy upon, from amongst His slaves, except the most righteous of them." [67]

---

[65] al-Bukhaaree, *Kitaabul-Adab* (The Book of Manners), in the chapter: "Showing mercy towards the child and kissing him and hugging him".
[66] al-Bukhaaree, *Kitaabul-Adab*, in the chapter: "Showing mercy towards the child and kissing him and hugging him".
[67] *Al-Adabul-Mufrad* (#99). Declared *saheeh* by *Shaykh* Al-Albaanee in *Saheeh Al-Adabul-Mufrad* [pg. 49, #72]

18 - From Yoosuf bin 'Abdullaah bin Salaam (☺), who said: "The Messenger of Allaah (ﷺ) named me Yoosuf, and he sat me on his lap, and rubbed my head." [68]

19 - Ya'laa bin Murrah (☺) reported: "We went out with the Prophet (ﷺ) and we had been invited for food, and Husayn was playing in the pathway. So the Prophet (ﷺ) hurried ahead of the people, then stretched out his hands rubbed him here one time and here another time, making him laugh, until he took him and put one of his hands on his chin and the other on his head, then embraced him and kissed him. Then the Prophet (ﷺ) said: **"Husayn is from me and I am from him. May Allaah love the one who loves al-Hasan and al-Husayn. Husayn is a sibt (nation) from the asbaat (nations) [in goodness]."** [69]

---

[68] *Al-Adabul-Mufrad* (#367). Declared *saheeh* by *Shaykh* Al-Albaanee in *Saheeh Al-Adabul-Mufrad* (pg. 107, #282)

[69] Declared *hasan* by *Shaykh* Al-Albaanee in *As-Saheehah* (#1227). →

20 - Usaamah bin Zayd (ﷺ) said: "The Messenger of Allaah (ﷺ) used to put me on (one of) his thighs and put al-Hasan on his other thigh, and then embrace us and say, *'O Allaah! Be merciful to them, for indeed I am merciful to them.'"*
70

21 - From Aboo 'Uthmaan, who said: Usaamah bin Zayd narrated to me: Once a daughter of the Prophet (ﷺ) sent a message to him, "Verily my child is going to die; please come to us!" So he sent the messenger back and told him to convey his greetings to her, and say, *"Verily for Allaah is whatever He takes, and whatever He gives is for Him, and*

→ **Benefit:** *Shaykhul-Islaam* Ibn Taymiyyah said: "And they (Ahlus-Sunnah) love *Ahlul-Bayt* (the members of the household) of the Messenger of Allaah (ﷺ), and show loyalty and allegiance to them, and they preserve the *wasiyyah* (will) of Allaah's Messenger (ﷺ) regarding them, when he said on the day of *Ghadeeru khumm*: *"I remind you of Allaah regarding my Ahlul-Bayt, I remind you of Allaah regarding my Ahlul-Bayt."* [Musim]." The *'aqeedah* of Ahlus-Sunnah is that we love and are loyal towards the members of the household of the Prophet (ﷺ), from his children, wives and relatives (ﷺ). And it is obligatory to follow their way, as the Prophet (ﷺ) said: *"O people! Indeed I left amongst you that which if you hold onto it you will never go astray – the Book of Allaah and the members of my household."* [See *as-Saheehah* (#1761)] And Ibnul-Malik said: "And the meaning of adhering to the members (of his household) is having love for them, and taking guidance from their guidance, way and lives." [see *Tuhfatul-Ahwadhee* (9/282)] And this shows the difference between those who adhere to the Truth and those who follow falsehood and innovation. The Raafidhah Shee'ah for example, they go to extremes in their love for 'Alee, Faatimah, al-Hasan and al-Husayn (ﷺ) and their descendants, to the extent that they call upon them and their "*imaam*s" as partners besides Allaah and ascribe to them what we don't even ascribe to the Messenger of Allaah (ﷺ) – and Allaah's refuge is sought! So our way is a way based upon the texts of the Book and the Sunnah and the guidance of the Companions, a way which is balanced and free from extremism and innovation.

70 al-Bukhaaree, *Kitaabul-Adab* in the chapter: "Placing the Child on the thigh". *Fath* (10/5789)

everything with Him has a limited fixed term (in this world): so be patient and hope for Allaah's reward." Then she again sent for him swearing that he should come to her; so he got up, and with him Sa'd bin 'Ubaadah, Mu'aadh bin Jabal, Ubayy bin Ka'b and Zayd bin Thaabit and some other men. So the child was lifted up to him, and the child's breath was disturbed (in his chest). He (the sub-narrator) said: I think he (Usaamah) said: as if it was a leather water-skin. So his eyes (the eyes of the Prophet ﷺ) started to shed tears. So Sa'd said, "O Messenger of Allaah! What is this?" So he said, *"It is mercy that Allaah has put in the hearts of His slaves, and Allaah is merciful only to those of His slaves who are merciful (to others)."* [71]

22 - Anas bin Maalik (ﷺ) said: Allaah's Messenger (ﷺ) said: *"There is not from amongst the people a Muslim, who three of his children die before the age of puberty, except that Allaah will enter him into Jannah due to His mercy towards them."* [72]

23 - Naafi' said: "Ibn 'Umar used to kiss his son Saalim when he would meet him, and say: 'A *shaykh* kissing a *shaykh*'." [73]

24 - Bukayr narrated that he saw 'Abdullaah bin Ja'far kiss Zaynab, the daughter of 'Umar bin Abee Salamah, and she was two years old or so." [74]

---

[71] al-Bukhaaree, *Kitaabul-Janaa'iz* (The Book of Funerals), chapter: The statement of the Prophet (ﷺ): *"The deceased is punished by..."*

[72] al-Bukhaaree, *Kitaabul-Janaa'iz*, "What is said regarding the children of the Muslims"

[73] *Kitaabul-'Iyaal* of *al-Imaam, al-Haafidh* Ibn Abeed-Dunyaa (#147)

[74] *Al-Adabul-Mufrad* (#365). Declared *saheeh* by *Shaykh* Al-Albaanee in *Saheeh Al-Adabul-Mufrad* [pg. 107, #280]

25 - Al-Ashja'ee said: "I saw Sufyaan [ath-Thawree] performing *hijaamah* (cupping) on his son, and the child was crying, and Sufyaan was crying due to his crying." [75]

26 - Muhammad bin Mas'adah al-Basree said: "Ja'far bin Muhammad had a son whom he loved deeply. So it was said (to him), 'to what extent has your love for him reached?' He said: 'I do not love that I have another son, so that my love (for my son) would spread to him [i.e. the other son].'" [76]

---

[75] *Kitaabul-'Iyaal* (#160)
[76] *Kitaabul-'Iyaal* (#156)

Good treatment towards ones Children and providing for them and fulfilling their Rights

27 – 'Abdullaah bin 'Umar (رضى الله عنهما) narrated that the Messenger of Allaah (ﷺ) said: *"Each one of you is a raa'ee (guardian), and each one of you is responsible for those under his charge. So the Imaam (Ruler) is a guardian and he is responsible for those under his care; a man is a guardian over his family and he is responsible for them; and a wife is a guardian over her husband's house and she is responsible (for it); a slave is a guardian for his master's wealth and property and he is responsible (for that). Beware! All of you are guardians and are responsible for those under his charge."* [77]

An-Nawawee said: "The scholars have said that the *raa'ee* is the guardian, the one who is entrusted, the one committed to the goodness and well-being of what he is responsible for, and what is under his supervision. So in it (this *hadeeth*) is that everyone who has something under his care and supervision, then it demands justice in it, and establishing what is

---

[77] Al-Bukhaaree in *Kitaabul-Jumu'ah*, *Kitaabul-Ahkaam*, *Kitaabul-Wasaayaa* and in *Kitaabun-Nikaah*, Chapter: **"Save yourselves and your families from a fire"**, Muslim in *Kitaabul-Imaarah*, Chapter: The virtues of a just ruler, and also by Ahmad, Aboo Daawood and at-Tirmidhee. See *Saheehul-Jaami'* (#4569).

beneficial to him in his *Deen* and his *Dunyaa* and those things related to him." [78]

28 – Anas (ﷺ) narrated that the Messenger of Allaah (ﷺ) said: ***"Verily Allaah will ask every guardian about those under his charge – was he heedful or was he neglectful – even asking a man about his family."*** [79]

29 – 'Abdullaah bin 'Amr (ﷺ) narrated that the Messenger of Allaah (ﷺ) said: ***"It is sufficient sin for a man that he neglect those whom he is responsible to provide for."*** [80]

30 – Al-Miqdaam bin Ma'adee Karib (ﷺ) reported that he heard the Messenger of Allaah (ﷺ) saying: ***"Whatever you feed yourself, then it is for you a sadaqah (charity), and whatever you feed your son, then it is for you a sadaqah, and whatever you feed your wife then it is for you a sadaqah, and whatever you feed your servant then it is for you a sadaqah."*** [81]

31 – Hakeem bin Hizaam (ﷺ) reported that the Prophet (ﷺ) said, ***"The upper hand is better than the lower hand (i.e. he who gives in charity is better than him who takes it), and start giving first to those you are responsible for. And the best sadaqah is that which is given by a wealthy person (from the money which is left after his expenses). And whoever abstains from asking others for financial help, Allaah will give him and save him from asking***

---

[78] *Sharh Saheeh* Muslim, *Kitaabul-Imaarah* (The Book of Leadership) (12/1829).

[79] *As-Saheehah* (#1636)

[80] Sunan Abee Daawood (#1692). Declared *hasan* by *Imaam* al-Albaanee. See *Saheehul-Jaami'* (#4481) and *al-Irwaa'* (#894)

[81] Declared *saheeh* by *Shaykh* al-Albaanee in *As-Saheehah* (#452)

others, and whoever asks Allaah to enrich him, Allaah will enrich him and make him self-sufficient." [82]

32 – Aboo Hurayrah (🙏) said: "The Messenger of Allaah (ﷺ) said: *'Give sadaqah!'* A man said: 'I have a *deenaar* (that I want to give in charity).' He said: *'Spend it (in charity) upon yourself.'* He said: 'I have another *deenaar*.' He said: *'Spend it (in charity) upon your wife.'* He said: 'I have another *deenaar*.' He said: *'Spend it (in charity) on your son.'* He said: 'I have another *deenaar*.' He said: *'Spend it (in charity) on your servant.'* He said: 'I have another *deenaar*.' He said: *'You are more (knowledgeable in regards to whom you should give it).'"* [83]

---

[82] Al-Bukhaaree in *Kitaabuz-Zakaah* (The Book of *Zakaah*)- Chapter: There is no *Sadaqah* except from the one who is wealthy.

[83] Collected by Ahmad in his *Musnad* (2/251), Aboo Daawood (#1691), an-Nasaa'ee (#2535), and it was declared authentic by Ibn Hibbaan (#3337) and al-Haakim (1/415), and Shaykh al-Albaanee declared it *hasan* in *al-Irwaa'* (3/408). It was also collected by ash-Shaafi'ee, al-Bayhaqee and al-Baghawee.

Benefit: If one were to look at these narrations from the Messenger of Allaah (ﷺ) in regards to *Sadaqah* and compare it to the way of the *Jamaa'aat as-Siyaasiyyah* (political groups and parties) of today, one can see that this affair is from those matters that distinguish the *da'wah* of *Ahlus-Sunnah* from the *da'wah* of all of those groups and parties. *Ahlus-Sunnah* follow the statement of the Messenger of Allaah (ﷺ), *"The upper hand is better than the lower hand."* and his saying, *"And do not ask the people for anything"* [Muslim]. So they do not ask the people for their wealth. Rather they spend from their own pockets upon their *da'wah*, and they begin by spending their *sadaqah* on their families first. As for the political groups and parties, then their collection boxes, bank allotments and asking the people for their *sadaqah* is their constant, inseparable characteristic. Rather it is from their most apparent traits! And it is the lifeline of their *da'wah*. So here the Messenger (ﷺ) was asked about giving a *deenaar* in *sadaqah*, and he (ﷺ) told him to spend it upon himself, then his wife, his children and then his servant before anyone else. But this is something you will never hear from the political groups and parties, because they support and base their *da'wah* upon *"the filth of the people"* [Muslim]. So if one were to ask them about a *deenaar* that he wished to give in *sadaqah*, they will never tell him to give it to →

33 – Jaabir bin Samurah (ﷺ) said: "I heard the Messenger of Allaah (ﷺ) say: *"If Allaah gives one of you something from goodness then let him begin with himself and his household."* [84]

34 - From Aboo Hurayrah (ﷺ): the Messenger of Allaah (ﷺ) said: *"The best Sadaqah is what is given when a person is wealthy, and the upper hand is better than the lower hand, and begin (in giving sadaqah) with those you are responsible for."* [85]

35 - From Aboo Sa'eed al-Khudree (ﷺ), that the Messenger of Allaah (ﷺ) said: *"There is no one who has three daughters, or three sisters, and he is good in his treatment of them, except that he enters Jannah."* [86]

36 - And it comes in the narration of Jaabir bin 'Abdillaah (ﷺ): "So a man from some of the people said: 'And two

---

→ anyone other than to their *hizb* (party)! And they use it in ways that strengthen their *hizb* and add to their numbers. So they will collect money for orphans and for students of knowledge to bring them close to their organization, to enlarge their group and strengthen it. Then this asking of the people is from their most apparent traits and the mainstay of their *da'wah*, whereas *Ahlus-Sunnah* spend from their own wealth to aid their *da'wah* and do not ask of the people. So then this matter is from those matters that distinguish the *da'wah* of *Ahlus-Sunnah* from all of the other *da'wah*s.

[84] Muslim in *Kitaabul-Imaarah* (the Book of Leadership), Chapter: "The people follow Quraysh", and Ahmad in *al-Musnad* (5/86, 88-89)

[85] Al-Bukhaaree in *Kitaabuz-Zakaah* (The Book of Zakaah)- Chapter: "There is no *Sadaqah* except for the one who is wealthy", Muslim in *Kitaabuz-Zakaah* by way of Hakeem bin Hazaam, an-Nasaa'ee in *Kitaabuz-Zakaah* (#2534 & 2543), Ahmad in his *Musnad* (2/278), al-Bayhaqee in *As-Sunan Al-Kubraa* (4/7862) and at-Tabaraanee in *Al-Mu'jam Al-Kabeer* (3/224)

[86] Declared *hasan* by Shaykh al-Albaanee in *As-Saheehah* (#294) and in *Saheeh Al-Adabul-Mufrad* (pg. 45, #59)

(daughters), O Messenger of Allaah?' He said: ***"And two."*** [87]

37 – Anas bin Maalik (ﷺ) said: "A woman came to 'Aa'ishah (رضي الله عنها), so 'Aa'ishah gave her three dates. Then she gave each of her children a date and kept one for herself. So the children ate the two dates and looked at their mother. So she took out the (last) date and split it (in two), then she gave each child half a date. Then the Prophet (ﷺ) came and 'Aa'ishah informed him (about that). So he said: ***"And what do you find so amazing about that? Indeed Allaah is merciful to her due to her mercy towards her two children."*** [88]

38 - Ibn 'Aa'ishah said: "it was narrated to me that Ayyoob [as-Sikhtiyaanee] used to say to his companions often: "Take a covenant of righteousness and goodness with your children and your family, and don't leave them (so that) their sight looks to the hands of the people (out of) desire."
He said: "And he had a basket that he carried to the market everyday, so he would buy fruits and the needs of his family and children."
He said: "And he [Ayoob] used to say: 'the best generosity is everything that I can gain reward for.'"
He said: "And Ayoob had in his household poor people, and he used to give them money and clothing by himself. So it was said to him: 'If only you would send it to them (instead of you taking it to them).'
He said: 'My going to them with it, to me, is more kind and compassionate to them.'" [89]

---

[87] Declared *hasan* by *Shaykh* al-Albaanee in *As-Saheehah* (#294 and #2492) and in *Saheeh Al-Adabul-Mufrad* (pg.45, #58)
[88] *As-Saheehah* (#3143), *Saheeh al-Adabul-Mufrad* (pg.47, #66)
[89] *Kitaabul-'Iyaal* (#379)

39 – Abool-Ahwas said: "I heard Sufyaan (ath-Thawree) say: 'Hold on to the work of heroes: earning from the *halaal* and spending upon the family." [90]

40 - Sa'eed binul-'Aas said: "If I teach my son the Qur'aan, and take him for Hajj and marry him off, then indeed I have fulfilled his rights, and then only my rights upon him remain." [91]

41 - Al-Hasan said: "The inhabitants of the heavens and the inhabitants of the earth do not know what Allaah gives the slave of reward due to something that by it, brings about happiness to his children, his family and his son." [92]

---

[90] *Kitaabul-'Iyaal* (#23)
[91] *Kitaabul-'Iyaal* (#312)
[92] *Kitaabul-'Iyaal* (#377)

Good treatment towards the Orphans and providing for them and taking care of their needs

42 – Allaah (ﷻ) said:

وَٱعْبُدُوا۟ ٱللَّهَ وَلَا تُشْرِكُوا۟ بِهِۦ شَيْـًٔا وَبِٱلْوَٰلِدَيْنِ إِحْسَٰنًا وَبِذِى ٱلْقُرْبَىٰ وَٱلْيَتَٰمَىٰ وَٱلْمَسَٰكِينِ وَٱلْجَارِ ذِى ٱلْقُرْبَىٰ وَٱلْجَارِ ٱلْجُنُبِ وَٱلصَّاحِبِ بِٱلْجَنۢبِ وَٱبْنِ ٱلسَّبِيلِ وَمَا مَلَكَتْ أَيْمَٰنُكُمْ ۗ إِنَّ ٱللَّهَ لَا يُحِبُّ مَن كَانَ مُخْتَالًا فَخُورًا

"Worship Allaah and join none with Him in worship, and do good to the parents, kinsfolk, and the orphans, *Al-Masaakeen* (the poor), the neighbor who is near of kin, the neighbor who is a stranger, the companion by your side, the wayfarer (you meet), and those (slaves) whom your right hands possess. Verily, Allaah does not like such as are proud and boastful." [93]

❈ *Shaykh* 'Abdur-Rahmaan as-Sa'dee said regarding this *aayah*:

---

[93] An-Nisaa' (4):36

"and the orphans"

"Meaning: those who lost their fathers and they are small, then they have a right upon the Muslims, whether they are relatives or other than them, with being taken care of and provided for, and being good to them, to comfort them, to instill good manners in them, to educate them with the best of education, in those things that are beneficial to their *Deen* (religion) and their *dunyaa* (worldly life)." [94]

43 - Sahl bin Sa'd (ﷺ) narrated that the Prophet (ﷺ) said: ***"I and the person who looks after an orphan and provides for him, will be in Jannah (Paradise) like this,"*** and he demonstrated by putting his index and middle fingers together." [95]

Al-Haafidh Ibn Hajr said: "His saying: **((I and the person who looks after an orphan))** meaning: the one who takes care of his affair and his well-being and benefit."
Al-Haafidh says: "And the meaning of his statement is that it he can be a grandfather, uncle, brother or the like of that from the relatives. Or it could be the father of the baby died so his mother takes his place. Or his mother died so his father takes on her place in education and nurturing. And al-Bazzaar brings from the *hadeeth* of Aboo Hurayrah in *mawsool* form [96]:

---

[94] See *Tayseerul-Kareemir-Rahmaan* (*Tafseerus-Sa'dee*)

[95] Al-Bukhaaree in *Kitaabul-Adab*, Chapter: "The virtue of taking care of an orphan", Muslim from Aboo Hurayrah in *Kitaabuz-Zuhd war-Raqaa'iq* (The Book of *Zuhd* and heart softening narrations)- Chapter: "Benevolent Treatment of the Widows, Orphans and the Poor". See *As-Saheehah* (#800).

[96] When the chain of narration is connected. This type of *hadeeth* is also called "*muttasil*". See *At-Tadhkiratu fee 'Uloomil-Hadeeth* of *al-Haafidh* Ibnul-Milqin (pg.15)

((Whoever looks after an orphan, a relative or a non relative of his)), and this narration explains the meaning of the narration that was before it."

And he goes on to mention: "Ibn Baṭṭaal said: It is a right upon the one who hears this *hadeeth* that he act by it so he can be the *rafeeq* (companion) of the Prophet (ﷺ) in *Jannah*, and there is no position in the Hereafter better than that." [97]

44 - Dhiyyaal bin 'Ubayd said: I heard my grandfather Handhalah say: I heard the Prophet (ﷺ) saying: **"There is no more** *(using the label of)* **orphancy (for him) when he reaches puberty, and there is no more orphancy for the young girl when she begins menstruating."** [98]

45 - Qatadah said: "Be towards the orphan like a merciful father, and reply to the *miskeen* with mercy and kindness." [99]

46 - Farqad as-Sabakhee said: "There has not been created a dinner table greater in nobility than the dinner table that the orphan eats from." [100]

47 - Asmaa' bin 'Ubayd said: "I said to Ibn Seereen, 'I have an orphan (so how should I be with him)?' He said: 'Do for him what you do for your own son, and spank him like you spank your own son." [101]

---

[97] *Al-Fath* (10/450-451)
[98] *As-Saheehah* (#3180)
[99] *Kitaabul-'Iyaal* (#616)
[100] *Kitaabul-'Iyaal* (#618)
[101] *Saheeh Al-Adabul-Mufrad* [pg. 57, #104]

Teaching Children *Tawheed* and the Correct *'Aqeedah*

48 - Ibn 'Abbaas (ﷺ) said: "I was behind the Messenger of Allaah (ﷺ) one day, and he said: *'O ghulaam (young man), I shall teach you some words [of advice]: Be Mindful of Allaah and Allaah will protect you. Be Mindful of Allaah and you will find Him in front of you. If you ask, then ask Allaah [Alone]; and if you seek help, then seek help from Allaah [Alone]. And know that if the Ummah were to gather together to benefit you with anything, they would not benefit you except with what Allaah had already prescribed for you. And if they were to gather together to harm you with anything, they would not harm you except with what Allaah had already prescribed (decreed) for you. The Pens have been lifted and the Pages have dried.'* " [102]

> *Shaykh* Ibn 'Uthaymeen said in his *Sharh al-Arba'een an-Nawawiyyah*: "**((O young man))** because Ibn 'Abbaas (رضي الله عنهما) was small, for indeed the Prophet (ﷺ) passed away and Ibn 'Abbaas was approaching puberty, meaning from fifteen to sixteen or less." [103]

---

[102] at-Tirmidhee (#2516) and *Shaykh* al-Albaanee declared it to be authentic

[103] Pg. 200

49 - Aboo Hafsah said: 'Ubaadah binus-Saamit (ﷺ) said to his son: "O my son! Indeed you will not find the sweetness of the reality of *Eemaan* until you know that whatever afflicts you was not going to miss you, and whatever missed you was not going to afflict you. I heard the Messenger of Allaah (ﷺ) say: ***"Indeed the first thing that Allaah created was the Qalam (The Pen), so He said to it 'Write!'. It said, 'O my Lord, and what should I write?' He said 'Write the decrees of everything until the Hour is established!'*** My son, I heard the Messenger of Allaah (ﷺ) say: "Whoever dies upon other than this then he is not from me." [104]

50 - Jundub bin 'Abdillaah (ﷺ) said: "We were with the Prophet (ﷺ) and we were youth who had grown strong (in body), so we learned *Eemaan* before we learned the Qur'aan, then we learned the Qur'aan and it increased us in *Eemaan*." [105]

51 – Mu'aawiyyah binul-Hakam as-Sulamee (ﷺ) narrated: "I had a slave-girl who tended my sheep by the side of Uhud and al-Jawwaaniyyah. So one day I came and found that a wolf had taken a sheep from her flock. And I am a man from the children of Aadam and become angry like they do, but I slapped her. So I came to the Messenger of Allaah (ﷺ) and he made me feel the seriousness of what I had done. I said: "O Messenger of Allaah, should I not set her free?" He (the Prophet) said: ***"Bring her to me."*** So I brought her to him, then He said to her: ***"Where is Allaah?"*** She said: "(He is) above the heavens." He said: ***"Who am I?"*** She said: "You are the Messenger of Allaah." He said: ***"Free her for she is a believer."*** [106]

---

[104] Aboo Daawood (#4700), at-Tahaawiyyah (#232) and *al-Mishkaat* (#94). Declared *saheeh* by *Shaykh* al-Albaanee

[105] Ibn Maajah (#61) and declared authentic by *Shaykh* al-Albaanee

[106] Muslim in *Kitaabus-Salaah* (The Book of Prayer) -Chapter: "The prohibition of speaking in the prayer".

52 - Muḥammad bin K̲h̲aalid bin 'Uthmaan reported from Maalik bin Anas that he said: "The *Salaf* used to teach their children love for Aboo Bakr and 'Umar, just like they would teach (them) a *soorah* from the Qur'aan." [107]

---

[107] al-Laalikaa'ee (#2325)

Teaching Children the Danger of Innovation in the *Deen* and Protecting them from it

❊ ❊ ❊

53 - Khuwayl, the brother-in-law of Shu'bah binul-Hajjaaj said: I was with Yoonus bin 'Ubayd, so a man came and said: "O Aboo 'Abdillaah! You forbid us from the gathering of 'Amr bin 'Ubayd [108], and your son has gone to him?" He (Yoonus) said: "My son?!" He said: "Yes." So Yoonus became angry. So I didn't leave until his son came, so he said: "O my son! You knew the opinion of 'Amr bin 'Ubayd, then you enter upon him?!" So he began to make excuses, so he said: "(But) So and so was with me!" So Yoonus said: "I prohibit fornication and stealing and drinking *khamr* (intoxicants), but for you to meet Allaah () with (all of) that is more beloved to me than you meet Him with the opinion of 'Amr bin 'Ubayd and the companions of 'Amr "– meaning

---

[108] 'Amr bin 'Ubayd bin Baab al-Basree, al-Mu'tazilee, al-Qadaree, from the heads of the Mu'tazilah and Qadariyyah and a caller to their innovated beliefs.

the Qadariyyah [109]. Sa'eed bin 'Aamir said: "We did not see any man who was better than him", meaning Yoonus (bin 'Ubayd). [110]

54 - Ma'mar said: "Ibn Ṭaawoos was sitting, then a man from the Mu'tazilah [111] came and he began to speak." He (Ma'mar) said: "So Ibn Ṭaawoos put his fingers in his ears." He (Ma'mar) said: "And he said to his son: 'O my son! Put your fingers in your ears! (Put them in) farther! Don't listen to anything from his speech!'" Ma'mar said: "Meaning, verily the heart is weak." [112]

---

[109] The Qadariyyah are a deviant sect founded by Ma'bad bin 'Abdillaah (or Khaalid) al-Juhanee in al-Baṣrah. From their false, innovated beliefs is their denial of Allaah's *Qadr* and His preceding knowledge of everything that would be before it came about, and that Allaah wrote all that would be before He created it. *Shaykhul-Islaam* Ibn Taymiyyah and others mention that this statement was the first of what was innovated into Islaam after the time of the Rightly-guided *Khulafaa'* and after Mu'aawiyyah bin Abee Sufyaan (ﷺ). Likewise they say that the human being creates his own actions. The Messenger of Allaah said about them: **"The Qadariyyah are the Magians of this Ummah."** [*ḥasan*: *Ṣaḥeeḥul-Jaami'* (#4442] al-Imaam al-Awzaa'ee said: "The first person to speak regarding (the denial) of *Qadr* was a man from the people of 'Iraaq called Sawsan [or it is said "Sansaweeh", or "Seenaweeh" or other than that], and he was a Christian who accepted Islaam, then returned to being Christian. Then Ma'bad al-Juhanee took it from him, and Gheelaan from Ma'bad." [*Kitaabush-Sharee'ah* of al-Aajurree (4/555)]

[110] *Al-Ibaanah* of Ibn Baṭṭah (#464)

[111] The Mu'tazilah are the followers of Waaṣil bin 'Aṭaa' al-Ghazaalee and 'Amr bin 'Ubayd. From amongst their innovated beliefs is that their denial of the *Ṣifaat* (Attributes) of Allaah. And the Mu'tazilah say that the person who commits the major sins is not a believer and not a disbeliever, but rather he is a state in between two states, and that the person who dies without having repented from the major sins will be in the Fire forever but his punishment will be less severe than that of the disbelievers.

[112] *Sharḥ Uṣool al-I'tiqaad* of al-Laalikaa'ee (1/247)

55 - It was said to Maalik bin Mighwal: "I saw your son playing with birds!" So he said: "How excellent that they distracted him from the companionship of an innovator." [113]

56 - Artaah binul-Mundhir said: "That my son be a *faasiq* from the *fusaaq* is more beloved to me than he be a person of desires [i.e. innovation]." [114]

57 - Hammaad bin Zayd said: "Yoonus (bin 'Ubayd) said to me: 'O Hammaad! Indeed if I were to see a youth upon every evil condition, then I do not despair of his goodness, until I see him accompany a person of *bid'ah*, for with that I know that he has been ruined." [115]

---

[113] *Ash-Sharhu wal-Ibaanah* of Ibn Battah (#90)
[114] *Ash-Sharhu wal-Ibaanah* (#87)
[115] *Ash-Sharhu wal-Ibaanah* (#94)

Benefit: The way of Ahlus-Sunnah is not to sit with, listen to or debate with *ahlul-bid'a* (the people of innovation) and to warn against them, as is clear in the books of the Salaf. And here we find the concern they had for the welfare of their children and the youth, fearing for them and warning them from innovation and it's people in order to preserve and protect their religion. You find that in every *khutbah* he would give, whether the *khutbah* of Jumu'ah or for a wedding or other than that, the Messenger of Allaah (ﷺ) would raise his voice and his face would turn red and he would say **"The most evil of affairs are the newly-invented affairs"**, but there was not one innovation! He repeated this over and over in every *khutbah* to ingrain this belief into the hearts of his Companions. Therefore, it is obligatory upon us to believe that innovation (*bid'ah*) is the most evil of affairs and to instill this belief into our children as well. →

→ And there are many narrations that show the evil and danger of innovation. For example, the Messenger (ﷺ) said: *"There will be a people who these ahwaa' (innovations) will flow through them just like rabies flows through the one who has been bitten. So there will not remain any joint except that it (innovation) enters into it."* [*Kitaabus-Sunnah* of Ibn Abee 'Aasim (#1)] And he said: *"Beware of the newly-invented affairs for indeed every innovation is misguidance."* [*Kitaabus-Sunnah* (#31)] Mu'aawiyyah narrated: *"Indeed this Ummah will divide into 73 sects due to innovation, all of them in the Fire except one, and it is the Jamaa'ah (the Companions)."* [*Kitaabus-Sunnah* (#2)] It is reported from Anas and Ibn 'Umar that the Prophet (ﷺ) said: *"Whoever desires other than my Sunnah then he is not from me."* [*Kitaabus-Sunnah* (#61 & 62)] He said (ﷺ): *"Indeed I have left you upon clear guidance, it's night is like it's day in clarity. No one deviates from it after me except that he is destroyed."* [*Kitaabus-Sunnah* (#48)] And the narrations from the Prophet (ﷺ), his Companions and those who followed after them in this issue are many.

Encouraging the Children upon Acts of Worship and Obedience

58 – Aboo Hurayrah (☬) reported that the Prophet (☬) said: *"There are seven whom Allaah will shade in His shade, on a day when there will be no shade but His shade: the just ruler, the youth who grows up (or is raised) in the worship of His Lord (and guards himself from His disobedience), and a man whose heart is attached to the masaajid, and two men who love each other for the Sake of Allaah, they meet due to it and part due to it, and a man who a woman of high status and beauty invites him (to commit fornication) so he says 'Verily I fear Allaah', and a man who gives in charity secretly, to the extent that his left hand does not know what his right is giving, and a man who remembers Allaah in private and so his eyes shed tears."* [116]

59 - 'Amr bin Shu'ayb reported from his father, from his grandfather, who said: The Messenger of Allaah (☬) said: *"Order your children with the Salaah at (the age of) seven, and spank them for (abandoning) it at ten, and separate them in the beds."* [117]

---

[116] Al-Bukhaaree in *Kitaabuz-Zakaah* (The Book of *Zakaah*) – Chapter: "Giving *Sadaqah* with the right hand", Muslim in *Az-Zakaah* – Chapter: "The virtues of concealing *Sadaqah*", at-Tirmidhee (#2391), and an-Nasaa'ee (#5380).

[117] *Sunan Abee Daawood* (#494) and *Shaykh* Al-Albaanee declared it *hasan saheeh*.

❀ Ibnul-Qayyim: "So in this *hadeeth* are three etiquettes: ordering them with it (the prayer), spanking them for (abandoning) it, and separation between them in the beds." [118]

60 - Khaalid bin Dhakwaan reported from ar-Rubayyi' bint Mu'awwidh bin Ghafraa' (ﷺ), who said: "The Messenger of Allaah (ﷺ) sent a messenger on the morning of 'Aashooraa' to the villages of the Ansaar that surround al-Madeenah: Whoever woke up fasting then let him complete his fast, and whoever woke up and wasn't, then let him complete the remainder of his day (without food). So after that we would fast it and make our small children fast, if Allaah willed. And we would go to the *masjid* and we would make toys out of wool for them, so when anyone of them felt hungry and cried for food, we gave him these toys until it was the time to break the fast." [119]

❀ An-Nawawee said: "And in this *hadeeth* is training the children upon acts of obedience and to get them used to acts of worship, but they have not yet reached the age of discernment and are not accountable for their actions." [120]

61 - Anas (ﷺ) said: "The Prophet (ﷺ) was the best of all the people in character, and I had a brother called Aboo 'Umayr." He (Anas) said: "I think he had been newly weaned. And

---

[118] *Tuhfatul-Mawdood*, pg.136

[119] al-Bukhaaree in *Kitaabus-Sawm* (the Book of Fasting), Chapter: "Fasting of Children", Muslim, Chapter: "The Recommendation for fasting on the Day of *'Aashooraa'* – Training the child upon acts of Obedience"

[120] *Sharh Saheeh Muslim, Kitaabus-Siyaam* (9/1136). Al-Haafidh Ibn Hajr mentions in *Fath*: "And the majority are upon (the opinion) that it is not obligatory upon whoever has not reached puberty. And a group from the *Salaf* have said it is desirable, from them Ibn Seereen and az-Zuhree. And ash-Shaafi'ee said this, that they order them with it (fasting) for training upon it if they are able to do it." *Fathul-Baree, Kitaabus-Sawm*, (4/1910)

whenever he came, he used to say, ***'O Aboo 'Umayr! What did al-Nughayr (the nightingale) (do)?'*** [121] He used to play with it, so sometimes the time of the Prayer would come while he (the Prophet) was in our house. So he would order that the carpet that was underneath him be swept and sprinkled with water, and then he would stand up (for the prayer) and we would line up behind him, and he would lead us in prayer. [122]

62 - Jaabir bin 'Abdillaah (ﷺ) said: "We were with the Messenger of Allaah (ﷺ) at 'Arafah, and a bedouin woman stuck her head out of her *hawdaj* [123], and with her was a small child, so she said: 'O Messenger of Allaah! Is there Hajj for this (child)?' He said: ***'Yes, and for you is the reward.'*** [124]

63 - As-Saa'ib bin Yazeed (ﷺ) said: "My father made me go for Hajj with the Messenger of Allaah (ﷺ) in the *Hajjatul-Wadaa'* (the Farewell Pilgrimage) and I was seven years old." [125]

---

[121] In other wordings collected by Ahmad and others it mentions that he used to play with this nightingale, until one day it died and the Messenger of Allaah (ﷺ) found him sad, so he rubbed his head and said what is reported in this narration. See *Fathul-Baaree* (10/5983)

[122] al-Bukhaaree, *Kitaabul-Adab*, chapter: "The *kunyah* for the child and before a child is born to a man."

[123] A litter with a canopy placed on the back of a camel in which a woman would ride.

[124] Muslim in *Kitaabul-Hajj*, Aboo Daawood (#1736), Ahmad (#219), and al-Bayhaqee in *as-Sunan al-Kubraa* (5/155 & 156) with various routes and wordings.

[125] at-Tirmidhee (#926) and declared *saheeh* by Shaykh al-Albaanee. At-Tirmidhee said: "And indeed the People of Knowledge have agreed that the child, if he makes Hajj before he reaches puberty, then it is upon him to make Hajj (again) when he reaches puberty, and that Hajj that he performed does not remove the Hajj of Islaam.... And it is the saying of Sufyaan ath-Thawree, ash-Shaafi'ee, Ahmad and Ishaaq."

64 - Ma'mar reported from az-Zuhree regarding the child, does one make Hajj with him? He said: "Yes, and he abstains from what the *muhrim* (the person in the state of *Ihraam*) abstains from, from clothing and perfume, and he doesn't cover his head, and the *jimaar* (pillars) are stoned by some of his family members on his behalf, and he is sacrificed for if he made *Tamattu'*." [126]

65 - Saalih bin Humayd said: "I saw al-Qaasim bin Muhammad undress his children (to put on the *Ihraam*) and he was ordering them to say the *Talbiyyah*." [127]

66 - Mu'aawiyah ibn Qura reported that his father used to say to his children right after they prayed *Salaatul 'Ishaa'*: "Oh my children, sleep. Perhaps Allaah will bless you with goodness by allowing you to stand a part of the night (in prayer)." [128]

---

[126] *Kitaabul-'Iyaal* (#651). *Tamattu'* is the type of Hajj when the pilgrim performs 'Umrah during the months of Hajj, and then enters Ihraam again on the 8th of Dhil-Hijjah to perform Hajj.
[127] *Kitaabul-'Iyaal* (#652)
[128] *Az-Zuhd* of *al-Imaam* Ahmad (pg. 234)

Encouraging the Children upon Seeking Knowledge

67 - 'Abdullaah bin 'Umar (رضي الله عنهما) narrated that Allaah's Messenger (ﷺ) said: ***"Verily amongst the trees there is a tree, the leaves of which do not fall off, and indeed it is the Muslim. So tell me, which (tree) is it?"*** So everybody started thinking about the trees of the desert." 'Abdullaah said: "And I thought that it was the date-palm tree, but felt shy (to answer). Then they said, "Tell us, which one it is, O Messenger of Allaah?" He replied: ***"It is the date-palm tree."*** 'Abdullaah said: "So I told my father what came to my mind. Then he said: *"That you had said it is more beloved to me than I have such and such."* [129]

In the wording of Muslim: *"That you had said it is the date-palm tree is more beloved to me than I have such and such."*

> ❈ *al-Haafidh* Ibn Hajr said: "And in it is respect for the elder, and the youth giving precedence to his father in speech, and that one does not rush with what he understood, even if he knows it to be correct. And in it is that the older scholar, it could be hidden from him what one who is less than him reaches, because knowledge is a blessing and Allaah gives His bounties to whomever He wills. And Maalik brought it as proof that the notions that occur in the heart

---

[129] Al-Bukhaaree in *Kitaabul-'Ilm* (The Book of Knowledge), Chapter: "*Al-Hayaa'* (shyness) in Knowledge", Muslim in *Kitaabu Sifaatul-Munaafiqeen wa ahkaamihim* (The Book regarding the characteristics of the Hypocrites), and at-Tirmidhee (#2867) and others.

from love of praise for (doing) good deeds are not reprehensible if their origin and basis was for Allaah (Alone). And that is derived from 'Umar's desire mentioned (in the *hadeeth*), and that 'Umar's desire (﷼) is what the human being has a natural tendency for, from love for goodness for himself and for his son, and that the virtue of the son in understanding become apparent in his youth, and so that he may increase in respect and status with the Prophet (ﷺ) and that perhaps he hoped that he would supplicate for him for an increase in understanding. And in it is an indication of the baseness and insignificance of the *Dunyaa* in the eyes of 'Umar, because he put the understanding of his son in one issue before red camels, [130] along with their great value and their expensive price." [131]

❁   An-Nawawee said: "And in it is the happiness of a person due to the excellence of his son, and the goodness of his understanding. And as for the statement of 'Umar (﷼), "*That you had said it is the date-palm tree is more beloved to me*", he intended by that that the Prophet (ﷺ) would supplicate for his son, and know the goodness of his understanding and his excellence." [132]

68 - Yahyaa bin Saalih al-'Abdee said: "I came to al-Hasan [al-Basree], and I was a youth, so I sat far away from the *halaqah* (circle of knowledge). So he said to me, 'O my son! Come closer. What did you sit so far away for?' He said: "I said 'O Aboo Sa'eed, indeed I have prepared my mat (to sit

---

[130] In the wording related by Ibn Hibbaan in his *Saheeh* (#243)
[131] *Al-Fathul-Baaree* (1/130)
[132] *Sharh Saheeh Muslim* (17/2811)

on).' ¹³³ He said 'Don't do that! When you come, then sit next to me.'" He said: "I would come to him and he would seat me at his side and rub my head and dictate *hadeeth* to me." ¹³⁴

69 - Sufyaan ath-Thawree said: "It is a must for a man to force his son to study the *Hadeeth*, for indeed he is responsible for him." ¹³⁵

70 - 'Abdullaah bin 'Ubayd bin 'Umayr said: "'Amr binul-'Aas stood at a circle (of knowledge) of Quraysh, and he said: 'What is wrong with you that you have cast aside these children? Don't do that! And make space for them in the gathering, and let them hear the *hadeeth* and make them understand it, for indeed they are the young ones of a people, and soon they will be the elders of a people. And you were (once) the young ones of a people, and today you are the elders of a people." ¹³⁶

71 - Zayd bin Akhzam said: "I heard 'Abdullaah bin Daawood say: 'It is a must for a man to force his son to listen to the *Hadeeth*'. And he used to say: 'The *Deen* is not by *kalaam* ¹³⁷, rather the *Deen* is only by the *aathaar* (narrations).'" ¹³⁸

---

¹³³ *Shaykh* al-'Anjaree explained that he was making an excuse to stay where he was, far away from the circle of al-Hasan, out of respect for the elders and due to his being young.

¹³⁴ *Kitaabul-'Iyaal* (#604)

¹³⁵ *Al-Hilyah* of Aboo Nu'aym (6/365)

¹³⁶ *Sharaf As-haabil-Hadeeth* of al-Khateeb al-Baghdaadee (#127), in the chapter "It is upon a man to force his son to listen to the *Hadeeth*."

¹³⁷ The innovation of using the intellect and theological rhetoric over the texts of the Book and the Sunnah, as *Shaykh* Ahmad as-Subay'ee explained.

¹³⁸ *Sharaf As-haabil-Hadeeth* (#128)

72 - Miskeen bin Bukhayr narrated that a man passed by al-'Amash and he was narrating *hadeeth*, so he said to him: "Are you narrating *hadeeth* to these children?!" So al-A'mash said to him: "These children are preserving your *Deen* for you." [139]

73 - Ibraaheem bin Adham said: "My father said to me: 'O my son! Seek after and study the *Hadeeth*. So every time you hear a *hadeeth*, and you have memorized it, you will get a *dirham*.' So I sought after and learned the *Hadeeth* upon that." [140]

74 - Luqmaan said to his son: "O my son! Do not learn what you do not know until you act upon what you already know." [141]

---

[139] *Sharaf As-haabil-Hadeeth* (#125)
[140] *Sharaf As-haabil-Hadeeth* (#131)
[141] *Iqtidaa'ul-'Ilmi wal-'Amal* of al-Khateeb al-Baghdaadee (#85)

Supplicating for the Children and Greeting them and Conveying *Salaam* to them

❈❈❈

75 – Allaah said:

وَإِذْ قَالَ إِبْرَاهِيمُ رَبِّ اجْعَلْ هَٰذَا ٱلْبَلَدَ ءَامِنًا وَٱجْنُبْنِى وَبَنِىَّ أَن نَّعْبُدَ ٱلْأَصْنَامَ ﴿٣٥﴾

"And (remember) when Ibraaheem said: O my Lord! Make this city (Makkah) one of peace and security, and keep me and my sons away from worshipping idols." [142]

 Al-Haafidh Ibn Katheer said regarding this verse: "It is upon every one who supplicates that he supplicate for himself and for his parents and for his offspring."

76 – Anas (✿) and others narrated regarding the Messenger of Allaah (✿) that: "When he would come to the homes of the Ansaar, the children of the Ansaar would come and surround him, and he would supplicate for them and rub their heads and give *salaam*s to them." [143]

---

[142] Ibraaheem (14):35

Benefit: the *Salaf* have explained that this *du'aa* of Ibraaheem (✿) for himself and his children shows the tremendous danger of *shirk* and the obligation of fearing it for oneself and ones family, as Ibraaheem at-Taymee said: "And who can feel safe from tribulation after Ibraaheem?" [*Ad-Durrul-Manthoor* (5/46)] So if Allaah's Messenger and *Khaleel* Ibraaheem (✿) feared shirk for himself and for his children, then what about us and our children?!

[143] Declared *hasan* by *Shaykh* al-Albaanee in *Adaabuz-Zuffaaf* [pg. 170]

77 — Anas (ﷺ) said: "The Messenger of Allaah (ﷺ) reached us and I was a young man amongst the youth, so he gave *salaam*s to us, then he took me by my hand and sent me with a message. And he sat in the shade of a wall, or he said against a wall, until I returned to him." [144]

78 - Shu'bah narrated from Sayyaar, who said: I was walking with Thaabit al-Bunaanee, so he passed by some children and he gave *salaam*s to them. So Thaabit said: "I was with Anas, and he passed by some children and he gave them *salaam*s. And Anas said: 'I was with the Messenger of Allaah (ﷺ), and he passed by some children and gave *salaam*s to them.'" [145]

> ❈ An-Nawawee said in *Sharh Muslim*: "In (this *hadeeth*) is the recommendation of giving *salaam*s to the children who are old enough to distinguish between right and wrong, and an encouragement towards humility, and spreading the *salaam* to all of the people, and a clarification of his humility (ﷺ) and the completeness of his compassion for all of the creation."

79 - Ibn 'Abbaas (رضي الله عنهما) narrated: The Prophet (ﷺ) used to seek Refuge with Allaah for al-Hasan and al-Husayn (by reciting):

---

[144] Aboo Daawood in his *Sunan* (#5203). Declared *saheeh* by *Shaykh* Al-Albaanee.

[145] Collected by al-Bukhaaree in *Kitaabul-Isti'dhaan* (The Book of Permissions) in the chapter "Conveying the *Salaam*s to the Children", Muslim in *Kitaabus-Salaam* in the chapter "The desirability of conveying the *Salaam* to the Children", Aboo Daawood (#5202-3) and at-Tirmidhee (#2696), and this is his wording and it was declared authentic by *Shaykh* al-Albaanee.

"I seek Refuge for you with the Perfect Words of Allaah from every shayṭaan and poisonous pest, and from every evil, harmful, envious eye."

In the wording of al-Bu<u>kh</u>aaree, he said (ﷺ): ***"Indeed your father** (Ibraaheem ﷺ) **used to seek refuge for Ismaa'eel and Is<u>h</u>aaq with it."***[146]

80 – 'Aa'ishah (رضي الله عنها) narrated that the Prophet (ﷺ) entered and he heard the voice of a child crying, so he said: ***"Why is this child of yours crying? Did you not make ruqyah for him from al-'ayn (the evil eye)?"***[147]

81 – Jaabir (ﷺ) reported that the Messenger of Allaah (ﷺ) said: ***"Do not make du'aa against yourselves, and do not make du'aa against your children..."***[148]

82 - Salamah bin Wardaan said: "I saw Anas bin Maalik shaking hands with the people, so he asked me: 'Who are you?' So I said: 'The freed slave of Banee Layth.' So he

---

[146] al-Bu<u>kh</u>aaree in his *Sa<u>h</u>ee<u>h</u>* in *Kitaabul-Anbiyyaa'*, At-Tirmi<u>dh</u>ee (#2060) and Aboo Daawood (#4737) and declared authentic by *Shay<u>kh</u>* al-Albaanee. The Arabic text is as follows:

((أُعِيذُكُمَا بِكَلِمَاتِ اللَّهِ التَّامَّةِ مِنْ كُلِّ شَيْطَانٍ وَهَامَّةٍ وَمِنْ كُلِّ عَيْنٍ لَامَّةٍ))

U'ee<u>dh</u>ukumaa bi kalamaatil-llaahit-taammati min kulli shayṭaanin wa haammatin wa min kulli 'aynin laammah

ﷺ Please note that أُعِيذُكُمَا (*U'ee<u>dh</u>ukumaa*) is for dual, as the Prophet (ﷺ) was reciting these words over both al-<u>H</u>asan and al-<u>H</u>usayn.
Benefit: Today we find Muslims who seek to protect their children from evil by hanging amulets around their necks and by other ways, and this is from making *shirk* with Allaah (ﷺ)! However the Muslim, the Sunnee, sticks to the Sunnah in seeking protection for his children.

[147] *As-Sa<u>h</u>ee<u>h</u>ah* (#1048)

[148] Declared *sa<u>h</u>ee<u>h</u>* by *Shay<u>kh</u>* al-Albaanee in *Sa<u>h</u>ee<u>h</u>ul-Jaami'* (#7267)

rubbed my head three times and said; *'BaarakAllaahu feek* (May Allaah bless you).'" [149]

---

[149] *Al-Adabul-Mufrad* (#966). Declared *saheeh* by *Shaykh* Al-Albaanee in *Saheeh Al-Adabul-Mufrad* [pg. 267, #747]

Kindness and Good Manners towards the Children and being patient with them

83 - Anas (﷠) reported that Allaah's Messenger (ﷺ) had the best manners of all the people. He sent me on an errand one day, and I said: "By Allaah, I will not go." But I had in my mind that I will go and do as the Prophet of Allaah (ﷺ) had commanded me to do. I went out until I came across some children and they were playing in the street. Then, Allaah's Messenger (ﷺ) came and he caught me by the back of my neck from behind me. He (Anas) said: So I looked up towards him and he was laughing. So he said: ***"O Unays (little Anas), did you go where I ordered you to go?"*** I said: yes, I'm going, O Messenger of Allaah." Anas further said: "I served him for nine years but did not know him to ever say for something that I had done 'why did you do that?', nor about a thing that I had left 'why did you not do that?'" [150]

---

[150] Muslim in *Kitaabul-Fadaa'il* (The Book of Virtues) (#2310)

84 - 'Aa'ishah (☺) narrated that the Messenger of Allaah (☺) put a child on his lap, performing *tahneek* [151] for him, and then the child urinated on him. So he called for water and then put it on (the place where the child had urinated). [152]

> ❀ *Al-Haafith* Ibn Hajr said: "And a benefit derived from it (this *hadeeth*) is gentleness with children and patience upon what occurs from them and not holding them responsible due to their not being at the age of discernment and accountability." [153]

85 - 'Uqbah binul-Haarith said: "I saw Aboo Bakr and he lifted al-Hasan and carried him and said, 'May my father be

---

[151] *Tahneek* was a custom among the Companions that whenever a child was born they used seek blessings by taking the child to the Prophet (☺) who would chew a piece of date and soften it with his saliva and then rub it inside the child's mouth. *Ash-Shaykh al-'Allaamah* Ahmad bin Yahyaa an-Najmee said: "And I do not see that they (the Companions) did that after the Prophet (☺) (passed away). For indeed they used to come with their children to the Prophet (☺) and he would perform *tahneek* on them and they did not do it- according to what I know- with Aboo Bakr, and not with 'Umar, and not with anyone other than them. So this proves their consensus on not seeking blessings from other than the Prophet (☺). So it is a must to not do it, and with Allaah lies the success." [*Fathur-Rabbil-Wudood* (2/369)]

[152] al-Bukhaaree, *Kitaabul-Adab* (The Book of Manners) in the chapter "Placing the Child on the lap".
Benefit: Aboos-Samh (☺) narrated that the Prophet (☺) said: **"Wash the urine of a small girl and sprinkle water for the urine of the small boy."** [an-Nasaa'ee (#304) and Ibn Maajah (#526) and declared authentic by *Imaam* al-Albaanee] The Permanent Committee mentioned in the 1st question from *fatwaa* #627: "Sprinkle (water on) the urine of the boy as long as he doesn't eat solid food. If he eats it, then he washes (the place where the urine is). And as for the girl, then he washes her urine off unrestrictedly, whether she eats food or doesn't eat food."

[153] *Fathul-Baaree* (10/5788)

sacrificed for you! (You) resemble the Prophet and not 'Alee', while 'Alee was smiling." [154]

---

[154] Al-Bukhaaree in *Kitaabul-Manaaqib*, Chapter "The virtues of al-Hasan and al-Husayn"

Justice between the Children

86 - From Anas (﷠) who said: A man was sitting with the Prophet (ﷺ), so his son came to him, so he took him then kissed him, then sat him on his lap. And a daughter of his came, then he took her to his side. So the Prophet (ﷺ) said: *"If only you were just between them."* [155]

87 - Haajib bin al-Mufadhdhal bin al-Mahallab narrated from his father, who said: "I heard an-Nu'maan bin Basheer say: The Messenger of Allaah (ﷺ) said: **'Be just between your children! Be just between your children! Be just between your children!'** [156]

88 - From Aboo Ma'shar, from Ibraaheem [an-Nakha'ee] (who) said: "They [the *Salaf*] used to prefer to be equal between their children, even in kissing (them)." [157]

89 - Layth narrated that al-Hasan (al-Basree) said: "If the teacher is not just between the children it is recorded as being from oppression." [158]

---

[155] *As-Saheehah* of *Shaykh* al-Albaanee (#2883 and 2994)
[156] *As-Saheehah* of *Shaykh* al-Albaanee (#1240)
[157] *Kitaabul-'Iyaal* (# 37)
[158] *Kitaabul-'Iyaal* (# 355)

Cultivating the Children upon Good Manners and Etiquettes

❊ ❊ ❊

90 – Mansoor binul-Mu'tamar said: "I heard regarding this *aayah*, from 'Alee:

$$\text{قُوٓا۟ أَنفُسَكُمْ وَأَهْلِيكُمْ نَارًا}$$

"Save yourselves and your families from a Fire (Hell)…" [159]

He said: 'Teach them and instill good manners in them.'" [160]

91 – Allaah () said:

$$\text{يَٰٓأَيُّهَا ٱلَّذِينَ ءَامَنُوا۟ لِيَسْتَـْٔذِنكُمُ ٱلَّذِينَ مَلَكَتْ أَيْمَٰنُكُمْ وَٱلَّذِينَ لَمْ يَبْلُغُوا۟ ٱلْحُلُمَ مِنكُمْ ثَلَٰثَ مَرَّٰتٍ ۚ مِّن قَبْلِ صَلَوٰةِ ٱلْفَجْرِ وَحِينَ تَضَعُونَ ثِيَابَكُم مِّنَ ٱلظَّهِيرَةِ وَمِنۢ بَعْدِ صَلَوٰةِ ٱلْعِشَآءِ ۚ ثَلَٰثُ عَوْرَٰتٍ لَّكُمْ ۚ لَيْسَ عَلَيْكُمْ وَلَا عَلَيْهِمْ جُنَاحٌۢ بَعْدَهُنَّ ۚ طَوَّٰفُونَ عَلَيْكُم بَعْضُكُمْ عَلَىٰ بَعْضٍ ۚ كَذَٰلِكَ يُبَيِّنُ ٱللَّهُ لَكُمُ ٱلْءَايَٰتِ ۗ وَٱللَّهُ}$$

---

[159] at-Tahreem (66):6
[160] Collected by al-Haakim in *al-Mustadrak* (2/494) and he declared it to be authentic and adh-Dhahabee agreed with him.

عَلِيمٌ حَكِيمٌ ۝ وَإِذَا بَلَغَ ٱلْأَطْفَٰلُ مِنكُمُ ٱلْحُلُمَ فَلْيَسْتَـٔذِنُوا۟ كَمَا ٱسْتَـٔذَنَ ٱلَّذِينَ مِن قَبْلِهِمْ ۚ كَذَٰلِكَ يُبَيِّنُ ٱللَّهُ لَكُمْ ءَايَٰتِهِۦ ۗ وَٱللَّهُ عَلِيمٌ حَكِيمٌ ۝

"O you who believe! Let those whom your right hands possess and those who have not reached the age of puberty to ask your permission (before they come to your presence) on three times; before *Fajr* (morning) prayer, and when you remove your clothes for the noonday (rest), and after the *'Ishaa'* (late-night) prayer. (These) three times are times of privacy for you. There is no sin upon you nor upon them after them (after those three times) to move about, attending to each other. Thus Allaah makes clear the *aayaat* (verses, signs) to you. And Allaah is All-Knowing, All-Wise. And when the children from among you reach puberty, then let them (also) ask for permission just like those senior to them (in age). Thus Allaah makes clear His *aayaat* for you. And Allaah is All-Knowing, All-Wise." [161]

> *Al-Haafidh* Ibn Katheer said: "So Allaah ordered the believers that their servants from what their right-hands possess and their children who have not reached puberty to seek permission (before entering upon them) in three situations: The first, from before *Salaatul-Ghadaah* (*Fajr*), because in that (time) the people are sleeping in their beds.

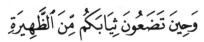

---

[161] An-Noor (24):58-59

"And when you remove your clothes for the noonday (rest)…"

meaning: in the time of *qayloolah* (mid-day nap), because a person may remove his clothes in that instance with his family.

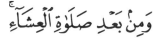

"And after the *'Ishaa'* (late-night) prayer."

Because it is the time of sleep. So the servant and children are ordered to not come upon the people of the house in these situations, due to what is feared of a man being in a state of intimacy with his wife, so Allaah ordered them to seek permission in these private times that Allaah named."

❖ *Shaykh* as-Sa'dee said: "That the master and the guardian (*walee*) of the small child are both addressed in regards to teaching their slaves and whoever is under their guardianship from the children, the knowledge and etiquettes legislated in the Sharee'ah, because Allaah directed the address to them by His saying:

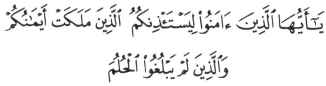

"O you who believe! Let those whom your right-hands possess and those who have not reached the age of puberty ask your permission (before they come to your presence)."

And that is not possible except by teaching them and cultivating them upon good manners, due to His saying:

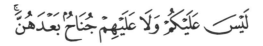

"There is no sin upon you nor on them after them (after those three times) to move about, attending to each other."

92 - 'Umar bin Abee Salamah said: "I was a youth in the lap of Allaah's Messenger (ﷺ) [162], and my hand was entering carelessly into the plate. So the Messenger of Allaah (ﷺ) said to me: *"O young man! Mention the name of Allaah, eat with your right (hand) and eat from what is in front of you."* Since then I have not ceased to apply those instructions (when eating)." [163]

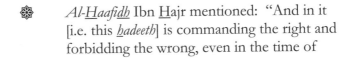 Al-Haafidh Ibn Hajr mentioned: "And in it [i.e. this hadeeth] is commanding the right and forbidding the wrong, even in the time of

---

[162] Al-Haafidh Ibn Hajr said in his explanation of this hadeeth: "Meaning, in his tarbiyyah and under his supervision, and that he nurtures him in his lap with the nurturing of a son." Fath (9/5376)

[163] Al-Bukhaaree in Kitaabul-At'imah (The Book of Foods), Chapter: Pronouncing the tasmiyyah over the food and eating with the right hand."

eating. And in it is the desirability of teaching the manners of eating and drinking." [164]

93 - From 'Anbasah bin 'Umaarah (who) said: Ibn 'Umar said to a man: "Hey you! Beautify your son's manners, for indeed you are responsible for him, and he is responsible for righteousness towards you." [165]

94 - Sufyaan said: "It used to be said, 'From the rights of the son upon the father is that he beautifies his manners.'" [166]

---

[164] It is upon us as parents to instill the proper *tarbiyyah* in our children, even in issues such as the manners of eating and drinking, for example. So we teach them to eat with the right hand and to eat from what is in front of them, not to talk while their mouths are full, and to withhold from burping and other basic manners. Likewise we must teach them bathroom manners and cleanliness, to clean up their rooms, and to keep themselves clean. Along with that they need to be taught respect for elders, truthfulness and so on. All of these things are from the *tarbiyyah* that we as parents must give to our children.
[165] *Kitaabul-'Iyaal* (#329)
[166] *Kitaabul-'Iyaal* (#332)

Marrying off ones Daughters

95 – Aboo Hurayrah (ﷺ) reported that the Messenger of Allaah (ﷺ) said: *"If someone comes to you whose character and religion pleases you then marry (her) to him. If you don't, there will be fitnah (trials and tribulations) in the land and corruption will become widespread."* [167]

96 – Aboo Moosaa (ﷺ) reported that he heard the Prophet (ﷺ) say: *"If a man wants to marry off his daughter, then let him seek her permission."* [168]

97 - Salamah bin Sa'eed narrated: A man said to al-Hasan [al-Basree]: "Verily I have a daughter, and she has been proposed to, so who should I marry her to?" He said: 'Marry her to someone who fears Allaah, for if he loves her, he will be good to her, and if he dislikes her, he will not oppress her." [169]

98 - Muhammad bin 'Abdur-Rahmaan bin Nufal reported that Asmaa' bint Abee Bakr said: "Marriage is bondage, so let one of you look to where he bonds his free one (his daughter) [170]" [171]

---

[167] At-Tirmidhee (#1084 & 1085), Ibn Maajah (#1967), al-Haakim (2/164), al-Bayhaqee (#13766) and others. Declared *hasan* by Shaykh al-Albaanee. See *As-Saheehah* (#1022) and *Al-Irwaa'* (#1868, 1926).

[168] Aboo Ya'laa in his *Musnad* (#1735) from Aboo Moosaa. Shaykh al-Albaanee said: "I say: And this chain is *saheeh*, its men, all of them are men of the *Saheeh* [i.e. Saheeh al-Bukhaaree]." See *As-Saheehah* (#1206).

[169] *Kitaabul-'Iyaal* (#125)

[170] Meaning that he should look to whom he gives his daughter to in marriage.

99 - Aboo Muslimah al-Minqaree said: "I heard Sallaam bin Abee Mutee' saying: 'I do not know it to be *halaal* (permissible) for a man to marry (his child) to a person of *bid'ah*, nor a person of *sharaab* (a person who drinks intoxicants). As for a person of *bid'ah*, then he causes his child to enter the Fire. And as for a person of *sharaab*, he will leave his child and not be concerned for him, and not teach (her), and he will do and he will do [i.e. he will fall into many sinful matters]'." [172]

100 - 'Abdul-'Azeez bin Qurayb said: "A man said to al-Ahnaf bin Qays: 'O Aboo Bahr! I do not see anyone who takes his time more than you.' He said: 'Know hastiness from me in three: the prayer when it comes in until I perform it, and the *Janaazah* (funeral) when it comes until I bury it, and the *ayyim* [173] if she is proposed to until I marry her off." [174]

---

[171] *Kitaabul-'Iyaal* (#118). Al-Bayhaqee said: "And that is reported in *marfoo'* form, and it being *mawqoof* is more correct. And Allaah (ﷻ) knows best." [see *As-Sunan al-Kubraa* (#13767]

[172] *Kitaabul-'Iyaal* (#123)

[173] *Ayyim*: a woman who has no husband, whether a virgin, a woman who has been married previously, or whether she was divorced or a widow. See *Lisaanul-'Arab* (1/290)

[174] *Kitaabul-'Iyaal* (#134)

Dealing with the Children during the Prayer

101 - Aboo Qataadah (☺) said: "The Prophet (ﷺ) prayed, and he was carrying Umaamah bint Zaynab. So when he bowed he put her down, and when he would stand up he picked her up." ¹⁷⁵

102 - From 'Amr bin Saleem, who narrated from Aboo Qataadah, that the Prophet (ﷺ) did that in *Salaatul-'Asr* (the *'Asr* prayer). ¹⁷⁶

103 - 'Abdullaah bin Mas'ood (☺) said: The Messenger of Allaah (ﷺ) was praying, so when he would prostrate, al-Hasan and al-Husayn hopped on his back. So when they wanted to prevent them (from that), he indicated to them to leave them alone. So then, when he completed his prayer, he put them

---

¹⁷⁵ Al-Bukhaaree in his *Saheeh*, *Kitaabul-Adab* (The Book of Manners) - Chapter: "Mercy towards the Child".
¹⁷⁶ *Kitaabul-'Iyaal* (#227).

Benefit: This narration shows that the Prophet (ﷺ) did that in the obligatory prayer, not the voluntary prayer as some claim. Likewise his carrying Umaamah, as *Shaykhul-Islaam* Ibn Taymiyyah mentions, is from those movements reported in the Sunnah that are allowed during the prayer for a benefit, like his order to kill the snake and the scorpion during the *Salaah*, his opening the door for 'Aa'ishah, his moving forward to prevent a woman from passing in front of him and his grabbing the shaytaan and choking him. [see *Majmoo'atul-Fataawaa* (22/560)] The noble *Shaykh* 'Ubayd al-Jaabiree mentioned that it is likewise allowed for the woman to move in order to prevent her child from touching something harmful, like a pot of hot food cooking on the stove [*'Umdatul-Fiqh* class in Kuwait, cassette #1].

both in his lap and said: ***'Whoever loves me, then let him love these two."*** ¹⁷⁷

104 - 'Abdullaah bin Abee Qataadah narrated from his father, Aboo Qataadah, that the Messenger of Allaah (ﷺ) said: ***"Indeed when I stand up in the Salaah, I want to elongate it, and I hear the crying of a child so I shorten my prayer out of dislike of making things difficult upon his mother."*** ¹⁷⁸

105 - And Shareek bin 'Abdillaah said: I heard Anas bin Maalik saying: "I never prayed behind any *Imaam* a lighter and more perfect prayer than that of the Prophet (ﷺ). And if he heard the crying of a child he would shorten the prayer out of fear of putting his mother to trial."

---

¹⁷⁷ *As-Saheehah* of *Shaykh* al-Albaanee (#312). *Shaykh* al-'Anjaree mentioned regarding this *hadeeth* that if this is what the Prophet (ﷺ) did during the prayer, with its great position and importance in Islaam, then imagine how the Prophet (ﷺ) was with children outside the prayer!

¹⁷⁸ Al-Bukhaaree in *Kitaabul-Adhaan* (The Book of the *Adhaan*), Chapter: "The one who lightens the Prayer due to the crying of a Child".

Allowing the Children to play

106 - 'Aa'ishah (رضي الله عنها) narrated: "The Messenger of Allaah (ﷺ) returned from the battle of Tabuk, or <u>Kh</u>aybar, and in her cubbyhole was a curtain. So a wind blew the curtain aside, exposing some dolls. He asked: *"What is this, O 'Aa'ishah?"* She replied "These are my dolls." And he saw amongst them a horse with wings made of leather, so he asked: *"What is this I see in the middle of them?"* She said "a horse". He said: *"And what is this on him?"* She said "two wings". He said: *"A horse with two wings?"* She said "Haven't you heard that Sulaymaan had horses with wings?" So he laughed until I saw his molar teeth." [179]

107 - Ibraaheem an-Na<u>kh</u>a'ee said: "They [the *Salaf*] used to allow the children (to play with) toys and games, all of them, except with dogs." [180]

---

[179] Aboo Daawood (#4932) and *Adaabuz-Zuffaaf* (170), declared *ṣaḥeeḥ* by *Shaykh* al-Albaanee.

Benefit: Some of the *'Ulamaa'* mention, as *Shaykh* al-'Anjaree explained, that the foundational principle in regards to children in these affairs is ease and leniency. We see in the case of 'Aa'ishah that she said that Sulaymaan (عليه السلام) had a horse with wings, and this would be rejected if a man [an adult] were to say this. But when 'Aa'ishah (رضي الله عنها) said it, the Prophet (ﷺ) laughed. This is one of the proofs that the scholars mention to show that the *aḥkaam* (rulings) related to children differ from those related to adults. And Allaah knows best.

[180] *Kitaabul-'Iyaal* (#597)

Keeping the Children inside at the time of Maghrib

108 – Jaabir bin 'Abdillaah (﷠) narrated that the Messenger of Allaah (ﷺ) said: *"Keep your children (inside) until the first part of the night goes, for indeed it is a time when the shayaaṭeen spread out."* [181]

109 – And he said (ﷺ): *"When the sun sets, keep your children (inside), for indeed it is a time when the shayaaṭeen spread out."* [182]

110 - And in the narration of 'Aṭaa' bin Abee Rabaaḥ, he said (ﷺ): *"…so if a period of time from the evening passes, then let them free (to go out)."* [183]

❂ *Shaykh* Ibn 'Uthaymeen (رحمه الله) was asked:
"If there is a courtyard attached to the house that the children play in within the confines of the walls of the house, then does the *hadeeth* of keeping the children inside at the time of Maghrib due to the *shayaaṭeen* spreading out apply to that, or does that apply to the street outside the house?"

---

[181] Al-Ḥaakim (4/284) and Aḥmad (3/362). Al-Ḥaakim said: "*Ṣaḥeeḥ* upon the conditions of Muslim" and adh-Dhahabee agreed with him. *Shaykh* al-Albaanee said: "And it is as they have said." See *Aṣ-Ṣaḥeeḥah* (#905)

[182] Aṭ-Ṭabaraanee in *Al-Mu'jam al-Kabeer* (3/26/2). It is supported by the following *hadeeth* as *Shaykh* al-Albaanee mentions in *Aṣ-Ṣaḥeeḥah* (#1366)

[183] See *Aṣ-Ṣaḥeeḥah* (#40)

The *Shaykh* answered: "The *hadeeth* is only regarding the street outside the house. And as for outside (within the confines of) the house, then there is no problem." [184]

---

[184] *Majmoo'atu as'ilati tahamal-usratil-Muslimah* of *Shaykh* Ibn 'Uthaymeen (pg. 151)

Verily among your Wives and your Children there are Enemies for you

111 - Allaah (ﷻ) said in His Book:

$$\text{يَٰٓأَيُّهَا ٱلَّذِينَ ءَامَنُوٓا۟ إِنَّ مِنْ أَزْوَٰجِكُمْ وَأَوْلَٰدِكُمْ عَدُوًّا لَّكُمْ فَٱحْذَرُوهُمْ ۚ وَإِن تَعْفُوا۟ وَتَصْفَحُوا۟ وَتَغْفِرُوا۟ فَإِنَّ ٱللَّهَ غَفُورٌ رَّحِيمٌ ۝}$$

"O you who believe! Verily, among your wives and your children there are enemies for you (i.e. may stop you from the obedience of Allaah), so beware of them! But if you pardon (them) and overlook, and forgive (their faults), then verily, Allaah is Oft-Forgiving, Most Merciful." [185]

❋ *Al-Imaam* Ibn Jareer aṭ-Ṭabaree mentions in his *tafseer* of this *aayah*: "He the Most High says, informing about the wives and the children (that) indeed from among them is the one who is an enemy to the husband and the father, with the meaning: that he diverts him from righteous actions, like His saying:

---

[185] At-Taghaabun (64):14

$$\text{يَٰٓأَيُّهَا ٱلَّذِينَ ءَامَنُوا۟ لَا تُلْهِكُمْ أَمْوَٰلُكُمْ وَلَآ أَوْلَٰدُكُمْ عَن ذِكْرِ ٱللَّهِ ۚ وَمَن يَفْعَلْ ذَٰلِكَ فَأُو۟لَٰٓئِكَ هُمُ ٱلْخَٰسِرُونَ}$$

"O you who believe! Let not your properties or your children divert you from the remembrance of Allaah. And whosoever does that, then they are the losers." [186]

So for this He said here:

$$\text{فَٱحْذَرُوهُمْ}$$

"so beware of them!"

Ibn Zayd said: meaning in regards to your *Deen*.

And Mujaahid said:

$$\text{يَٰٓأَيُّهَا ٱلَّذِينَ ءَامَنُوٓا۟ إِنَّ مِنْ أَزْوَٰجِكُمْ وَأَوْلَٰدِكُمْ عَدُوًّا لَّكُمْ}$$

"O you who believe! Verily, among your wives and your children there are enemies for you."

He said: he leads a man to cutting off the ties of kinship or to disobedience to His Lord. So a man is

---

[186] Al-Munaafiqoon (63):9

not able, along with his love for him [i.e. the one whom he loves], to obey him." [187]

❁   Ash-Shanqeeṭee said: "And from what is considered Qur'aanic advice and direction towards remedying the problems of married life and the issue of the children, He follows it with His saying, the Most High:

"But if you pardon (them) and overlook, and forgive (their faults), then verily, Allaah is Oft-Forgiving, Most Merciful."

Meaning: indeed the enmity of the wife and children, one should not meet it except with pardoning, excusing and forgiveness. And that lightens, removes or prevents the husband and the father from the results of this hostility, and that it is better than arguing and disputing." [188]

---

[188] *Adwaa'ul-Bayaan*

A Final Note from Ibnul-Qayyim

Al-Imaam Ibnul-Qayyim (رحمه الله) said:

"And some of the People of Knowledge have said: Verily Allaah سبحانه will ask the father about his son on *Yawmul-Qiyaamah* before he will ask the son about the father. For indeed just as the father has a right upon his son, so the son has a right upon his father, as He said – the Most High:

قُوٓاْ أَنفُسَكُمۡ وَأَهۡلِيكُمۡ نَارًا وَقُودُهَا ٱلنَّاسُ وَٱلۡحِجَارَةُ

"O you who believe! Save yourselves and your families from a Fire (Hell) whose fuel is men and stones." [189]

'Alee bin Abee Ṭaalib said: *"Teach them and instill in them good manners."* And He said – the Most High:

وَٱعۡبُدُواْ ٱللَّهَ وَلَا تُشۡرِكُواْ بِهِۦ شَيۡـًٔا وَبِٱلۡوَٰلِدَيۡنِ إِحۡسَٰنٗا وَبِذِى ٱلۡقُرۡبَىٰ

"Worship Allaah and do not join any partners with Him in worship, and do good to parents and kinsfolk…" [190]

---

[189] At-Taḥreem (66):6
[190] An-Nisaa' (4):36

And the Prophet (ﷺ) said: *"Be just between your children".* So the advice and bequest of Allaah for the fathers towards their children precedes the advice and bequest of the children towards their fathers. Allaah the Most High said:

"And do not kill your children out of fear of poverty..." [191]

So whoever neglects teaching his child what will benefit (him), and leaves him fruitlessly, then he has harmed and wronged him with the utmost harm. And most of the children, their corruption only comes by way of the fathers and their negligence of them, and abandoning teaching them the obligatory matters of the *Deen* and its *sunan*. So they waste and squander them while they are small. So they (the children) do not benefit themselves, nor do they benefit their fathers when they become old. And just as some of them (the parents) admonish their child for disobedience and not being dutiful (to them), then he (the child) likewise says: 'O my father! Indeed you were careless and undutiful towards me when I was small, so now I am careless and undutiful towards you when you have reached old age. And you neglected me as a child, so I have neglected you as an old man.'" [192]

---

[191] Al-Israa' (17):31
[192] *Tuhfatul-mawdood bi ahkaamil-Mawlood* (pg. 139)